TECHNOLOGY INTEGRATION
IN THE
ELEMENTARY MUSIC CLASSROOM

TECHNOLOGY INTEGRATION

IN THE
ELEMENTARY MUSIC CLASSROOM

by Amy M. Burns

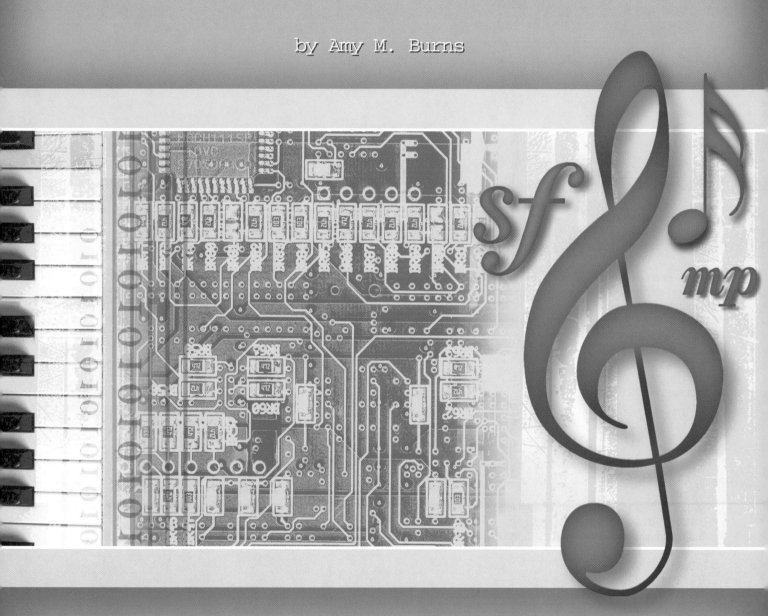

ISBN-13: 978-1-4234-2757-5
ISBN-10: 1-4234-2757-2

Published by:
Hal Leonard Corporation
7777 W. Bluemound Road
P.O. Box 13819
Milwaukee, WI 53213

Library of Congress Cataloging-in-Publication Data

Burns, Amy M.
  Technology integration in the elementary music classroom /
by Amy M. Burns. -- 1st ed.
      p. cm.
  Includes bibliographical references and index.
  ISBN 978-1-4234-2757-5
  1. School music--Instruction and study. 2. Educational
technology--Planning. I. Title.
  MT10.B894 2007
  372.87'044--dc22
                                        2007043516

Printed in the U.S.A.

First Edition

Visit Hal Leonard Online at **www.halleonard.com**

CONTENTS

Introduction

How would you answer the following question:

How can music technology benefit the elementary level (grades K–6)?

At one point in my career, I would have answered the above question with the following statement: "Technology cannot possibly benefit elementary music classes." I would have answered the question this way for two reasons: (1) elementary students are too young to use technology, and (2) I don't have the time to learn how to use or utilize technology in an elementary classroom with one computer. However, if I gave these answers today, this book would never have been written. I have been teaching music at the primary grade level for 12 years, and I now answer the question with the following resounding exclamation: "Technology can and will benefit your elementary general music classroom!" Why did I change my opinion? Because I have learned through first-hand experience that technology, if used appropriately, can enhance elementary music classes by reaching those students who are musically gifted, those students who appreciate music, and those students who act out continuously during music class.

Elementary students are growing up in an age of technology. Students between the ages of 5 and 11 do not fear technology because they most likely own and use one or more of the following: a portable MP3 player or CD player, an Xbox or a Nintendo Wii, or a DVD player or VCR. This became evident to me while I was conducting research for my capstone research project to complete my Master of Science in Music Education from Central Connecticut State University. I focused on composition with music technology at the elementary level. When I asked one of my Kindergarten and one of my third grade general music classes, "What is this item?", all of the students in both classes answered, "It's an iPod!" They were correct. They all knew that this small, hand-held, white device was the iPod that I use to play musical excerpts, accompaniments, and listening examples for music class. I then asked the Kindergarten music class of 16 students how many of them had a family member that owns an iPod. Fifty-five percent (55%) of the class answered that their siblings, parents, relatives, or they themselves own an iPod. When I asked my third grade music class of 14 students the same question, 78 percent answered that their siblings, parents, relatives, or they themselves own an iPod and that they use it on a daily basis.

RESEARCH

Technology is becoming more visible and easier to use, especially at the younger ages. Reese, McCord, and Walls (2001) support this view based on the findings of a survey they gave to students ages 10–17. The researchers discovered that 78 percent of students have a computer at home. Of those who responded, 57 percent use the computer every day, 88 percent use a computer to do school work, and 73 percent have access to the Internet (Reese, McCord, & Walls 2001, 1).

Technology is everywhere in our culture, and it has literally become an integral part of the day-to-day life for educators, musicians, and consumers (Rudolph 2004, 1; Swearingen 2003, 114; Rudolph, Richmond, Mash, & Williams 1997, 1). In addition, Dr. Thomas Rudolph (2004) suggests that the implementation of technology into the elementary general music classroom should be based on the belief that technology will enhance the learning process, rather than being the driving force of the entire music curriculum (p. 11). I agree with this and feel that technology is a wonderful classroom tool—an instrument that can be used to improve classroom learning and to successfully address every student's learning style. Technology is also a powerful tool promoting the development of high levels of skill and understanding of creative thinking and problem-solving with music (Reese, McCord, & Walls 2001, 4). The findings of research conducted by the Yamaha Corporation related to the use of technology in music education were also very positive. The results of one study revealed that students who received hands-on instruction had greater comprehension of musical concepts compared to students taught with traditional approaches and methods (Rudolph 2004, 4–5). Furthermore, my own research for my master's degree also definitively proved that technology can enhance students' learning of basic musical skills in an elementary music classroom.

The purpose of my study (*Music Technology Will Enhance Composition Skills in Grade Two*) was to test the hypothesis that music technology can enhance composition studies in the second grade music classroom at Far Hills Country Day School in Far Hills, New Jersey. The study specifically focused on standard number four (composing and arranging music within specified guidelines) of the nine National Association for Music Education (MENC) K–12 National Standards. I assigned one second grade music class to be the control group (N=15), another second grade music class to be experimental group 1 (N=15), and another second grade music class to be experimental group 2 (N=15). The control group was taught the fundamentals for basic music skills through traditional methods such as singing songs, performing on instruments, movement, and speech. Experimental group 1 was taught the fundamentals for basic music skills through the same traditional methods, along with composing a four-measure melody using traditional materials such as notation, manuscript paper, and a pencil. Experimental group 2 also learned the fundamentals for basic music skills through traditional methods. However, students in this group were taught composition with the aid of music technology, such as Harmonic Vision's Doodle Pad, Apple's GarageBand 2 and Finale Music's Finale NotePad 2005. All groups received thirty minutes of instruction twice a week for ten weeks. A pre- and post-test was administered to determine if the use of technology improved the learning of music fundamentals.

The results of the pre- and post-tests showed that there was a significant statistical difference of improvement ($p<.05$) for all three groups (see Fig. 2). However, experimental group 2 showed the greatest increase of correct answers from the pre-test to the post-test, whereas experimental group 1 showed the least increase. Experimental group 2, which used traditional methods to learn basic music skills and then utilized technology to create a composition, resulted in a 48 percent increase of correct answers from the pre-test to the post-test. The control group, which was taught basic music skills through traditional methods but did not compose during the study, showed a 46 percent increase in correct answers. This was a significant increase in correct answers from the pre-test to the post-test, but this was to be expected because the entire 20 lessons of the control group was devoted to learning basic music skills without composing. In contrast, experimental group 1, which was taught basic music skills through traditional methods and utilized those skills to compose a song traditionally (with manuscript paper and a pencil), demonstrated the smallest increase with a 16.7 percent increase of correct answers. Therefore, the hypothesis that lessons enhanced with the aid of music technology can improve retaining music skills being taught was accepted.

Note: I feel compelled to state that although my research was conclusive, it may not apply to your particular situation. The study would have to be adapted to your situation in order for it to be relevant to you.

Group	Pre-Test	Post-Test	+ or -	d	rd
EX1	89	115	+	26	1
CG	59	128	+	69	2
EX2	62	135	+	73	3

Note: + or - = use for sign test; *d* = difference; *rd* = rank of difference.

Fig. 2: Results of questions answered correctly on the pre- and post-test for all three groups.

Research indicates students who become active participants in learning gain confidence, learn more effectively, and are drawn to further study (Rudolph, Richmond, Mash & Williams 1997, 1). Technology *is* a tool that gives students the hands-on instruction that produces greater comprehension of musical concepts. It also promotes confidence and effective learning (Rudolph, Richmond, Mash & Williams 1997; Reese, McCord & Walls 2001). However, we must remember that technology is just that: a tool— it cannot replace teachers. Technology cannot replace how we encourage our students to continue to try, to achieve, and to succeed at new concepts and skills. It cannot be a substitute for the ways in which we give students the knowledge to learn new information and the power to use that knowledge to better their daily lives. In addition, technology will never replace how we develop relationships with our students as their coaches, their mentors, their counselors, and their friends. As Peter Webster states in *Computer-Based Technology and Music Teaching and Learning* (1992, p. 435),

> "So, is music technology effective and is it worth the trouble? On balance and on a very basic level, the answer to this question is yes. Does music technology hold the key for solving all our music teaching problems? Of course not. Are there abuses in its use? Absolutely. Does it always improve learning? No, much depends on the context—especially the teacher and its use instructionally. Is it worth the trouble to keep studying its role in music teaching and learning? Unconditionally, yes."

This book is a resource for elementary general music teachers who wish to enhance their curriculums with music technology. It is my hope that music teachers will utilize music technology as teaching tools to allow students to engage and manipulate the basic concepts of music.

HOW CAN THIS BOOK ASSIST AN ELEMENTARY MUSIC TEACHER?

As mentioned earlier, technology is here to stay and, when used appropriately, has enhanced teaching in the elementary general music classroom. As elementary music teachers, we strive to give our young students hands-on musical experiences, which help students learn and retain information better than when traditional methods of music teaching—including books, paper, and pencil—are used. Activities such as using classroom instruments, sound sources, movement activities, play activities, and finger plays are just a few examples of teaching tools that music teachers use to create musical hands-on experiences. As Rudolph states in his book *Teaching Music with Technology* (2004), music technology and music education can be compared with the colorful creative tools of crayons, paints, and markers of an art class. Rudolph sees music technology as an artistic tool for music that can enhance the music curriculum and meet the standards of music organizations including the National Association for Music Education (MENC), the International Society for Technology in Education (ISTE), and the Technology Institute for Music Educators (TI:ME) (Rudolph 2004, 7).

The lesson plans in this book help elementary general music teachers to enhance their current curriculum with the hands-on tools of music technology. If you are teaching a lesson that involves form, then "Creating Music within a Specified Form" would be an excellent choice. Alternatively, if you need to reinforce the teaching of the 12-bar blues progression, then Dr. Rudolph's "12-Bar Blues Accompaniment" will assist greatly. As you look to improve your current curriculum, you can use or adapt the lesson plans in this book as a way to motivate and facilitate optimal learning for elementary students. Including technology within instructional formats provides multiple opportunities to increase student learning. Whether you are a novice or advanced technology user, whether you have one computer in your music room, you teach "a la cart," or you teach in a lab, you can easily enhance your elementary general music lessons with the addition of technology, as demonstrated in the lesson plans included in this book.

LESSON PLAN FORMAT

The lessons presented in this book were gathered from music educators who have contributed lessons to the Technology Institute for Music Educators (TI:ME) website (http://www.ti-me.org) or to the periodical *Music Education Technology* (http://metmagazine.com/), as well as music educators who have created them on their own, such as TI:ME 2006 Teacher of the Year Karen Garrett (http://musictechteacher.com). The music educators who contributed to this book have successfully utilized these lessons in their own music classrooms.

The lessons are designed to be used in an elementary music classroom for grades Kindergarten through six. They can be adapted and used in a general music classroom setting with one computer or in a music class taught in the elementary classroom setting where the music teacher transports his/her music materials on a cart. The lessons can also be adapted and used in a keyboard lab (a room that has multiple electronic keyboards with or without computers) or in a computer lab (a lab with multiple computers that is usually available for use by the entire school).

These lessons are labeled according to the teacher's technical ability. Therefore, each lesson has the rating of novice, intermediate, and advanced so that a teacher using these lesson plans will be able to identify his/her own level of technological comfort. The descriptions for the ratings are as follows:

Novice—The teacher is able to utilize the computer, to install and/or download software, is able to work the mouse, and is able to launch and run basic commands in a word processing and notation software program. The teacher can operate a CD player and an electronic keyboard. The teacher is also able to connect the computer to an LCD projector, TV screen, and/or Smart Board (an interactive whiteboard system) for demonstrational purposes. The teacher is also able to access the Internet.

Intermediate—The teacher can perform all of the activities stated above. In addition, the teacher can compose, edit, and arrange with notation software. Furthermore, he/she is comfortable recording with a digital audio device, using digital audio software and/or music production software, and burning CDs. The teacher can utilize and teach with an electronic keyboard and/or keyboard lab, and can access and play MIDI files. The teacher can also access, utilize, and teach with educational sites on the Internet. In addition, the teacher has the ability to create and print work sheets using notation or word processing software.

Advanced—The teacher can perform all of the activities stated above. In addition, the teacher can publish his/her website for his/her own or educational purposes, record and publish audio files and/or students' works to a CD and/or website, and create podcasts (a method of publishing audio files to the Internet allowing users to subscribe to a feed and receive new files automatically by subscription). The teacher can utilize a program that creates animation, such as Flash. The teacher can use a digital camera or video camera and knows how to create and burn DVDs. The teacher can also connect and use an electronic MIDI device to sequence music and accompaniments for classroom and concert purposes.

The lessons are also organized so that the teacher can easily see which of the nine MENC National Standard(s) is being addressed and which area of technology as defined by TI:ME is being utilized. At the beginning of each lesson plan, there is a box that lists the MENC standards and the TI:ME technology areas addressed. In addition, the lessons provide the teacher with information about materials, duration, prior knowledge, procedure, evaluation, and examples of how to follow up the lesson.

There are also handouts and files to accompany many of the lessons so that you do not need to make them on your own. Lesson materials such as an accompaniment, a work sheet, a PowerPoint file, a MIDI file, a notation file, and/or an audio file can be found on the TI:ME website (http://www.ti-me.org/TIEMC/). This link will bring you to a page that will have all of the handouts, MIDI files, notation files, and audio files so that you can easily download them onto your computer. The files have the following extensions: audio files (extension .mp3), MIDI files (.mid), Finale notation files (.mus), Sibelius notation files (.sib), and portable document format files (.pdf). If the lesson requires the audio files, you can download them onto your computer and play them on your computer's audio player. For PCs, this is most likely Microsoft Windows Media Player, Apple's iTunes, or Apple's Quicktime Player. For Macs, this is most likely Apple's iTunes or QuickTime Player. If a lesson requires a MIDI file, you can download the MIDI file and open it with any notation, sequencing, or digital audio software such as Finale, Sibelius, Cakewalk Sonar Home Studio, Apple's GarageBand, MOTU's Digital Performer, Digidesign's Pro Tools, and so forth. If the lesson requires a notation file, then you have a few choices. The notation files that need to be edited as a part of the lesson were saved as Finale, Sibelius, and MIDI files. Therefore, if you own Finale, you can open the Finale notation file (.mus); if you own Sibelius, you can open the Sibelius notation file (.sib). If you do not have either of these notation programs, or you have older versions of these programs, then you can open the notation file that was saved as a MIDI file (.mid). Lesson work sheets that need to be printed are presented as pdf files on the website. A pdf file requires Adobe Acrobat Reader (http://www.adobe.com/products/acrobat/readstep2.html) so that it can be opened and read. The PowerPoint file (.ppt) requires Microsoft PowerPoint (http://office.microsoft.com/powerpoint) in order to run.

This book also contains a glossary and an index. The glossary lists definitions of terminology used in the lesson plans. For example, if you are not familiar with sequencing but you would like to utilize a lesson that involves it, you can look up the definition in this section. In addition, it gives you definitions of basic technology terminology. Furthermore, the index lists each lesson by page number, grade level, MENC standard, and TI:ME technology area covered.

In conclusion, enhancing your instruction with technology can result in every student engaging and learning in the elementary general music class. As music teachers, this is one of our top priorities. I hope that this book will provide you with some helpful ways to increase, facilitate, and motivate students' learning with technology.

PART 1

TECHNOLOGY-ENHANCED LESSON PLANS
THAT EMPHASIZE MUSICIANSHIP BY ADDRESSING THE MENC
STANDARDS 1, 2, AND 3:

1. Singing, alone and with others, a varied repertoire of music.
2. Performing on instruments, alone and with others, a varied repertoire of music.
3. Improvising melodies, variations, and accompaniments.

MENC Standards:	1. Singing, alone and with others, a varied repertoire of music.
	6. Listening to, analyzing, and describing music.
TI:ME Technology Areas:	4. Instructional music software
	5. Multimedia
	7. Internet

Singing the Melodic Direction of the Letters *V* and *W* Using Morton Subotnick's creatingmusic.com

By Amy M. Burns
Far Hills Country Day School, Far Hills, New Jersey

Grade Level:	Kindergarten
Teacher's Technical Ability:	Novice
Objective:	The kindergartners will be able to sing the melodic direction of the letters *V* and *W* with the assistance of Morton Subotnick's website, http://www.creatingmusic.com.
Materials/Equipment:	• Markers (or crayons).
	• Paper.
	• Slide whistle.
	• One computer connected to a TV.
	• Smart Board or an LCD projector.
	• Pictures of the letters *V* and *W* (you can make these pictures or access them on the TI:ME website: http://www.ti-me.org/TIEMC.
	• Morton Subotnick's website: http://www.creatingmusic.com.
Duration:	30 minutes
Prior Knowledge and Skills:	The kindergartners know how to draw the letters capital *V* and *W* and have experienced singing the melodic directions of high to low and low to high.
Procedure:	1. Review the letters *V* and *W* by having the students identify the letters from the pictures. You can draw the letters or use the pictures on the TI:ME website.
	2. Hand out blank papers and markers (or crayons) and have the students write the letters.
	3. Introduce or review the melodic direction of the letters by playing the melodic direction of each letter on a slide whistle and then having the students echo-sing each letter.
	4. Add movements to show the melodic direction of the letters.
	5. Have the students sit in front of the TV, screen, or Smart Board as you launch http://www.creatingmusic.com.
	6. Click on "Musical Sketch Pads" (see Fig. 1.1).

Musical Sketch Pads

Fig. 1.1: Morton Subotnick's creating music.com.

7. Click on "Sketch Pad" (see Fig. 1.2).
8. Using the pencil tool, write the letter *V* (see Fig. 1.3).
9. Click on the play button and listen to the letter *V*.
10. Ask the students if that sounded like what they heard, sang, and moved to before. It should be familiar enough for them to recognize it.
11. Have them sing along and move with the melodic direction of the letter *V* being played from creatingmusic.com.
12. To erase the letter, click on the square tool, highlight the letter *V*, and click on the pencil eraser.
13. If your students can operate a mouse, have one of the kindergartners draw the letter *W* and click to listen to the letter *W*.
14. Have the students continue with additional letters in the alphabet, and have the students describe the melodic direction using words such as high, low, stays the same, etc.

Fig. 1.2: Sketch Pad.

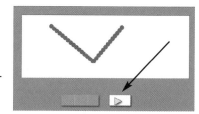

Fig. 1.3: The arrow is pointing to the play button.

Evaluation: This lesson permits the evaluation of the Kindergarten class as a whole, as opposed to individually evaluating the students. The following rubric was devised to evaluate the class as a whole:

	Singing the melodic direction of the letter *V*	Singing the melodic direction of the letter *W*
Excellent	All of the students participate and correctly sing the melodic direction of the letter *V*.	All of the students participate and correctly sing the melodic direction of the letter *W*.
Good	75 percent–95 percent of the students participate and correctly sing the melodic direction of the letter *V*.	75 percent–95 percent of the students participate and correctly sing the melodic direction of the letter *W*.
Fair	50 percent–74 percent of the students participate and correctly sing the melodic direction of the letter *V*.	50 percent–74 percent of the students participate and correctly sing the melodic direction of the letter *W*.
Novice	Below 50 percent of the students participate and correctly sing the melodic direction of the letter *V*.	Below 50 percent of the students participate and correctly sing the melodic direction of the letter *W*.

Follow-up: A follow-up lesson is to have the kindergartners write their names using paper, markers (or crayons), and then use http://www.creatingmusic.com to listen, sing, and move to the melodic direction of their names.

Items to Be Purchased: If you have a computer that can connect to a TV, Smart Board, or screen, and your computer has Internet access, then you will not need to purchase any items for this lesson.

Download from www.ti-me.org/TIEMC: "W.pdf" and "V.pdf"

MENC Standards:
1. Singing, alone and with others, a varied repertoire of music.
2. Performing on instruments, alone and with others, a varied repertoire of music.
6. Listening to, analyzing, and describing music.
7. Evaluating music and musical performances.

TI:ME Technology Areas:
2. Music production

"Hey Diddle Diddle!"
By Amy M. Burns
Far Hills Country Day School, Far Hills, New Jersey

Grade Level: K–2

Teacher's Technical Ability: Intermediate

Objective: The students will sing, act, and perform on Orff instruments to the nursery rhyme "Hey Diddle Diddle!" In addition, the students will have their performance recorded so that they can assess themselves.

Materials/Equipment:
- The nursery rhyme "Hey Diddle Diddle!" composed with the pitches sol, la, and mi (see below and on the TI:ME website).
- Audio recording software such as Audacity, GarageBand, or Cakewalk Sonar Home Studio (see "Items to Be Purchased").
- Scarves, puppets, or plush animals to represent the cat, cow, moon, dog, dish, and spoon.

Duration: 30 minutes

Prior Knowledge and Skills: The students will need to know how to hold the mallets of an Orff instrument and be able to sing the pitches sol, mi, and la.

Procedure:
1. Introduce the song "Hey Diddle Diddle!" (see Fig. 1.4 and "Download from www.ti-me.org/TIEMC" below).
2. Echo-sing the song and have the students repeat what you sing.
3. Sing the song together.
4. Act out the song:
   a. Assign one student to be the cat (you can use a scarf, a puppet, or a plush cat for the student to hold so that it identifies him/her as the cat).

Fig. 1.4: "Hey Diddle Diddle." This can also be found on the website as a full-size version.

4

Procedure: b. Assign another student to be the cow, one to be the moon, one to be the dog, one to be the dish, and one to be the spoon.

c. Have those students act out the song, while the other students sing the song.

d. Take turns until all students have had a turn.

5. Orffestration:

   a. If you are performing this lesson with Kindergarten or first grade, I usually just have them play the steady beat together on alternating C and C' bars. If you are doing this lesson with second graders, you can have them play both parts (see letter 5d.).

   b. Have the students tap the steady beat on their legs, alternating between left and right.

   c. Transfer this pattern to the Orff instruments by playing it on the notes C and C' (I have them alternate the bars, but you can also have them play the steady beat on both bars together).

   d. To play in two parts, I would have the xylophones play the steady beat pattern on the two Cs and the glockenspiels play a "zing" (running the mallet across the notes from low to high) on the words "moon" and "spoon."

   e. If you do not have enough Orff instruments for all of the students, have some students play the Orffestration, some students sing the melody, and some students act out the song.

6. Recording the melody:

   a. When I tell my students that I will be recording them playing the Orff instruments and singing, the students will immediately sit up, play with all of the proper mallet technique, and play with all of the correct notes and rhythms. They love to hear themselves recorded.

   b. Launch Apple's GarageBand, create a new project, and then create a new real instrument track (press the +, then click on "Real instrument").

   c. Press the record button (the red button on the bottom of the screen), and record the students playing. Make sure to turn off the metronome by clicking on the "Control" menu and scrolling down to "Metronome" (or "Apple u").

   d. Once recorded, play back the recording and have the students listen for their parts, voices, and/or steady beat.

   e. Save this recording so that at the end of the year, you will have a compilation CD of their Orffestrations to play back for them. This is always fun for them to hear because they will reminisce about playing the instruments and singing the songs.

Evaluation: The following rubric can be used to assess the objectives in this lesson:

	The students can sing "Hey Diddle Diddle!" in tune (pitches sol, mi, and la).	The students can play the Orffestration correctly.
Excellent	The students can sing the song in tune with no assistance from the teacher.	The students can play the steady beat with no assistance from the teacher.
Good	The students can sing the song in tune with little assistance from the teacher.	The students can play the steady beat with little assistance from the teacher.
Fair	The students have a difficult time singing the song in tune but can achieve success with much assistance from the teacher.	The students have a difficult time playing the steady beat but can achieve success with much assistance from the teacher.
Novice	The students cannot sing the song in tune even with assistance from the teacher.	The students cannot play the steady beat even with assistance from the teacher.

Follow-up: This lesson can be followed up with other lessons that Orffestrate, sing, and act out nursery rhymes. In addition, when they perform more Orffestrations and songs, you can record them using GarageBand and eventually compile them all on one CD. At the end of the school year, you can play the CD for them and remind them of all of their musical ventures for that school year.

Items to Be Purchased: This lesson can be performed using relatively inexpensive recording audio software such as Apple's GarageBand (http://www.apple.com/ilife/garageband/), or Cakewalk Sonar Home Studio (http://www.cakewalk.com/Products/DAWs.asp). Please note that Apple offers educator's discounts. This lesson can also be performed using the freeware Audacity (http://audacity.sourceforge.net/).

Download from www.ti-me.org/TIEMC: "Hey_Diddle_Diddle.pdf"

MENC Standards:	1. Singing, alone and with others, a varied repertoire of music.
	6. Listening to, analyzing, and describing music.
TI:ME Technology Areas:	1. Electronic instruments
	2. Music production

Making a Round/Canon Come Alive with Technology

By Amy M. Burns
Far Hills Country Day School, Far Hills, New Jersey

Grade Level: K–2 (or any elementary grade level that can sing rounds)

Teacher's Technical Ability: Intermediate to advanced

Objective: The students will be able to sing and identify their part of a round.

Materials/Equipment:
- Simple rounds such as "Frère Jacques," "Row, Row, Row Your Boat," "Make New Friends," etc.
- A computer that is connected to a TV screen or an LCD projector.
- Sequencing program.
- Electronic keyboard.

Duration: 20 minutes

Prior Knowledge and Skills: The students can sing a round successfully and comprehend the definition of a round.

Procedure:
1. Before the lesson, sequence the melody line of a round and show this in graphic notation (advanced technical ability). You do this by inputting the melody line using an electronic keyboard. Or, you could download a round from a website, then open it up in a sequencer that shows it in graphic notation (intermediate technical ability).
2. When the students arrive, introduce or review the round with the students.
3. They all sing the round together in unison.
4. You then divide the students into sections so that they can sing the round in two parts.
5. Have the students sit in front of the screen and listen to the computer play the round as they view each part on the graphic/piano roll of the sequencer (see Fig. 1.5).

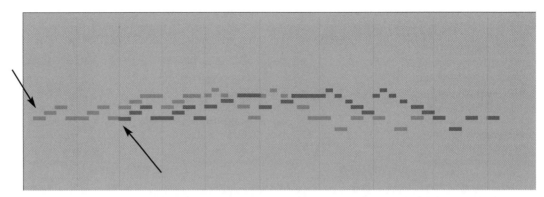

Fig. 1.5: Here is a MIDI file of "Frère Jacques" in Digital Performer. The left arrow points to where part 1 begins, and the right arrow points to where part 2 begins. If you were to look at this on a computer screen, part 1 is red and part 2 is blue. As the file plays, the students will listen to the file and look at the parts to determine which color represents their part. I downloaded this MIDI file from the Internet. The only change I had to make was to modify the color of the second part to blue. It was originally a different shade of red.

      6. The students must identify which color is their part.
      7. The students then sing along with the sequencer in parts.

Evaluation: The students will be able to sing the round in parts. In addition, they will be able to listen to and identify their specific part.

Follow-up: Once the students have mastered singing and identifying two parts, you can expand the song into a three- to four-part round. This would require you to cut and paste the melody into a new track to produce a three-part round, and cut and paste the melody into an additional track to produce a four-part round.

Items to Be Purchased: If you have a computer in your classroom, then you will need to purchase a sequencing program. A novice sequencing program can be fairly inexpensive (Cakewalk Sonar Home Studio for PC or Intuem for Mac). For those desiring a more costly, professional sequencing/digital audio program, consider Pro Tools, which currently runs on both PC and Mac, or MOTU's Digital Performer, which is for Mac only).

Download from www.ti-me.org/TIEMC: None

MENC Standards:	K–4 standards:

K–4 standards:
2. Performing on instruments, alone and with others, a varied repertoire of music.
3. Improvising melodies, variations, and accompaniments.
6. Listening to, analyzing, and describing music.
8. Understanding relationships between music, the other arts, and disciplines outside the arts.

Pre-K standards:
1. Singing and playing instruments.
2. Creating music.
3. Responding to music.

TI:ME Technology Areas: 5. Multimedia

"Let's Go Find a Bear" with a Digital Video Presenter

By Amy M. Burns
Far Hills Country Day School, Far Hills, New Jersey

Grade Level: Pre-K–1

Teacher's Technical Ability: Novice

Objective: The students will act out the movements of the story and improvise sound effects to the sounds that occur in the story using voices, body percussion, and/or classroom instruments.

Materials/Equipment:
- *We're Going on a Bear Hunt*, by Michael Rosen (author) and Helen Oxenbury (illustrator), published by Little Simon; Board edition, October 1, 1997 (see Fig. 1.6).
- Elmo video projector (see Fig. 1.7). Elmo is a digital visual presenter that allows you to present images of virtually anything to anyone at any time. As you act out the book, you can place the book on the Elmo, hook it up to an LCD projector, and it will project the page onto a wall or screen. This means that you do not need to make transparencies of each page of the book or try to find

Fig 1.6: Michael Rosen's and Helen Oxenbury's We're Going on a Bear Hunt.

the big book version of the book. You can just put the book on the Elmo and it will be projected beautifully by the LCD projector.

- An LCD projector connected to Elmo.
- A screen or wall to project onto.
- Classroom instruments (optional).

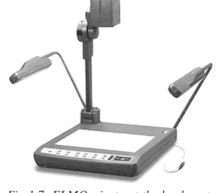

Fig 1.7: ELMO—just put the book on top of the presenter, and with the aid of an LCD projector, it will project onto a wall or screen. No need for transparencies or the big book.

Duration: 30 minutes

Prior Knowledge and Skills: The students do not need to have any prior knowledge or skills for this lesson.

Procedure:
1. Read the book to the students.
2. Read the book again and act out the movements. In order to see the book while the students are acting it out, place it on the Elmo and let it project onto a wall or screen.
3. As you read the book for the third time, use voices, body percussion, and/or classroom instruments to make the sound effects printed in the book. Again, put the book on the Elmo with the LCD projector connected to it, so that it projects onto a wall or screen.

Evaluation: The students will comprehend the story by acting it out and by using their voices, body percussion, and/or classroom instruments to make the sound effects.

Follow-up: This lesson could be integrated into a unit about animals or a unit about literature.

Items to Be Purchased: The Elmo (http://www.elmousa.com/presentation/index.html) and the LCD projector are pricey items that should be purchased using a school budget, not a music budget. However, there are different types of these products that are more adaptable to a school budget.

Download from www.ti-me.org/TIEMC: None

MENC Standards:	2. Performing on instruments, alone and with others, a varied repertoire of music.
TI:ME Technology Areas:	4. Instructional software

Can Recorder Drills Be Fun? Yes!

By Amy M. Burns
Far Hills Country Day School, Far Hills, New Jersey

Grade Level:	3–6
Teacher's Technical Ability:	Novice
Objective:	The students will be able to successfully practice and perfect the performance of the notes B, A, and G above middle C on the recorder.
Materials/Equipment:	• PG Music's Band-in-a-Box software (http://www.pgmusic.com). • Computer with speakers. • Recorders.
Duration:	10 minutes
Prior Knowledge and Skills:	This lesson assists the teacher with fingering and note drills on the recorders. The only prior knowledge and skills the students would need are how to play B, A, and G above middle C on the recorder. The teacher would need to know how to open the Band-in-a-Box application and enter chord symbols.
Procedure:	1. Before the class begins, open the application Band-in-a-Box on your computer. 2. Type in the chord symbol "G" and click "Enter." 3. Click "Play." The song will now play a G chord for 32 measures, three times in a row, in a jazz style, through the computer's speakers. 4. When the students enter, pass out the recorders and explain to the students that they will be imitating different rhythmic patterns using the notes B, A, and G. 5. Click "Play" on the computer and have them echo what you play. You can play various patterns of the note B, A, or G. In addition, you could play numerous patterns with all three notes. 6. Evaluate the students' hand positions, fingerings, and breath control so that they do not "pop" the note G to the higher octave. 7. When the students tire of the jazz style, click on the "S" menu and change the style (see Fig. 1.8).

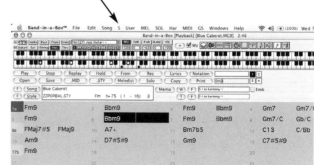

Fig. 1.8: Changing styles in Band-in-a-Box.

Evaluation: Since this lesson can produce various levels of achievement, the following rubric has been made to clarify assessment:

	Performing the note B	Performing the note A	Performing the note G
Excellent	The students can perform the note B with the proper hand position, fingerings, and breath support all of the time.	The students can perform the note A with the proper hand position, fingerings, and breath support all of the time.	The student can perform the note G with the proper hand position, fingerings, and breath support all of the time.
Good	The students can perform the note B most of the time with the proper hand position, fingerings, and breath support.	The students can perform the note A most of the time with the proper hand position, fingerings, and breath support.	The student can perform the note G most of the time with the proper hand position, fingers, and breath support.
Fair	The student can perform the note B some of the time with the proper hand position, fingerings, and breath support.	The students can perform the note A some of the time with the proper hand position, fingerings, and breath support.	The student can perform the note G some of the time with the proper hand position, fingerings, and breath support.
Novice	The students cannot perform the note B without popping the note.	The students cannot perform the note A without popping the note.	The student cannot perform the note G without popping the note.

Follow-up: This lesson can be followed up with the same preparation, but this time, the teacher improvises a two-measure "question" on the recorder using the notes B, A, and G. The students then respond with an improvised two-measure answer that must end on the note G. This lesson can also be done on various instruments such as keyboards, Orff instruments, stringed instruments, and classroom percussion instruments (straight rhythm patterns, no notes). Band instruments may be used as well, but I recommend using a B♭ chord in BIAB and having the instruments improvise on concert D, C, and B♭.

Download from www.ti-me.org/TIEMC: If you do not have Band-in-a-Box but your computer can play an audio file, you will find the audio files for this lesson on the website: "Recorder_Drill_Jazz.mp3" or "Recorder_Drill_Rock.mp3."

MENC Standards:	2. Performing on instruments, alone and with others, a varied repertoire of music.
	3. Improvising melodies, variations, and accompaniments.
	4. Composing and arranging music within specified guidelines.
	9. Understanding music in relation to history and culture.
TI:ME Technology Areas:	1. Electronic instruments

Drumming with Keyboards

By Dr. Thomas E. Rudolph
Haverford School District, Haverford, Pennsylvania

This article was previously published in the June 2004 issue of *Music Education Technology* magazine, a property of Penton Media, and is reprinted with the permission of its publisher.
http://metmagazine.com/mag/drumming_keyboards/

Grade Level: Grades 4–6

Teacher's Technical Ability: Novice (if you use a CD accompaniment track)
Intermediate (if you use a MIDI track accompaniment)

Objective: To develop the ability to play in time, listening skills, and explore rhythmic improvisation.

Materials/Equipment:
- Electronic keyboards.
- CD tracks or standard MIDI files.

Duration: Three activities for three class periods

Prior Knowledge and Skills: The prior knowledge needed for this lesson is basic keyboard skills, such as turning on the keyboard and pressing the keys.

Procedure: **Activity 1**

1. The first step is exploring the percussion sounds in your synthesizers. If a synthesizer is compatible with General MIDI (GM), then its drum sounds are already mapped or assigned to specific MIDI Note Numbers (see the table "GM Level 1 Percussion Map"); that means they are set up to respond to a keyboard. Check the user manual to be sure; it usually includes a list of the specific drum sounds that your synth can produce. To understand MIDI Note Number assignments, remember that 60 is the MIDI Note Number for middle C, the C♯ above middle C is 61, and so on.

2. When my students explore the percussion sounds on their keyboards, I ask them to find the locations of the ride cymbal (assigned to MIDI Note 51), bass drum (Note 36), snare drum (Note 38), and low, middle, and high tom-toms (Notes 47, 48, and 50).

3. After students become familiar with the locations of drum sounds, I have them play along with a prerecorded accompaniment such as a CD track or a standard MIDI file. I encourage them to select any percussion sound they like for accompanying

the track, and to try to imitate the drum part on the track. I also choose songs in a specific form, such as ABA with eight-measure phrases. This form allows students to vary patterns and enter drum fills within the appropriate measure.

Activity 2

1. Once students are comfortable playing along with a track, I introduce a basic drum pattern.
2. First, students select GM program 129 (on many Korg keyboards this is GM program 129) or GM drums (a set of percussion sounds, mapped across the keyboard). The left hand plays the bass and snare drum parts. Using GM percussion, this could be notated and played with the second and third fingers on the left hand.
3. When students are comfortable playing along with the snare and bass, I have them add the ride cymbal pattern with the right hand, playing only quarter notes at first.
4. Next, I ask them to double the cymbal pattern with the right hand. I ask them to play the first pattern with section A of the recording and change to the second pattern for section B.
5. The final step is playing a drum fill on the last measure of each eight-measure phrase.
6. After students become familiar with basic drum patterns, they can improvise variations. One fun activity is to have them bring in recordings and try to imitate the drum parts and fills that they hear.

Activity 3

Teachers are always in search of new, fun, educational activities, and learning to create drum parts is all of that and more. Once your students get into the groove, you can teach rhythms from around the world using the ethnic percussion sounds in your synthesizers, thus meeting MENC National Standard 9, which asks you to demonstrate the relationship between music and culture.

GM Level 1 Percussion Map
(60 = Middle C)

Note#	Drum Sound	Note#	Drum Sound	Note#	Drum Sound
35	Acoustic Kick	51	Ride Cymbal 1	67	High Agogo
36	Kick 1	52	Chinese Cymbal	68	Low Agogo
37	Side Stick	53	Ride Bell	69	Cabasa
38	Acoustic Snare	54	Tambourine	70	Maracas
39	Hand Clap	55	Splash Cymbal	71	Short Whistle
40	Electric Snare	56	Cowbell	72	Long Whistle
41	Low Floor Tom	57	Crash Cymbal 2	73	Short Guiro
42	Closed Hi-Hat	58	Vibraslap	74	Long Guiro
43	High Floor Tom	59	Ride Cymbal	75	Claves
44	Pedal Hi-Hat	60	High Bongo	76	High Wood Block
45	Low Tom	61	Low Bongo	77	Low Wood Block
46	Open Hi-Hat	62	Mute High Conga	78	Mute Cuica
47	Low-Mid Tom	63	Open High Conga	79	Open Cuica
48	High-Mid Tom	64	Low Conga	80	Mute Triangle
49	Crash Cymbal 1	65	High Timbale	81	Open Triangle
50	High Tom	66	Low Timbale		

Evaluation: The more you teach about percussion and rhythm using a MIDI keyboard and drum-sound source, the more possibilities you will discover. I intersperse percussion lessons throughout the school year while keeping the following goals in mind: to develop the ability to play in time, to develop listening skills, and to explore rhythmic improvisation.

Follow-up: **Do the keyboard synthesizers in your lab lack percussion sounds?**
If so, you have some alternatives. You could purchase inexpensive GM keyboards that include a bank of percussion sounds. Another option is purchasing MIDI sound modules that include percussion sounds.

Computer labs with MIDI keyboards

If your lab has computers connected to MIDI keyboards, you can also try one or more software synthesizers. For example, Propellerhead Software's Reason (http://www.propellerheads.se/) (Mac/Win) includes a pattern-based software drum machine called Redrum, which offers 78 drum kits. You can also choose from a variety of specialized drum programs, such as Steinberg Groove Agent (Mac/Win) and Native Instruments Battery (Mac/Win).

Another alternative

With auto-accompaniment programs such as PG Music's Band-in-a-Box (Mac/Win) (http://www.pgmusic.com), you can access built-in percussion sounds using the computer's alphanumeric keyboard.

Download from
www.ti-me.org/TIEMC: None

MENC Standards:	2. Performing on instruments, alone and with others, a varied repertoire of music.
	5. Reading and notating music.
	6. Listening to, analyzing, and describing music.
	7. Evaluating music and musical performances.
	8. Understanding relationships between music, the other arts, and disciplines outside the arts.
TI:ME Technology Areas:	1. Electronic instruments

Teaching Dynamics

By Don Muro

Detailed lesson plans on dynamics and other elements of music are included in Don Muro's MIDI keyboard curriculum.
For more information, please visit:
http://www.donmuro.com/curriculum.htm
This article was previously published in the February 2006 issue of *Music Education Technology* magazine,
a property of Penton Media, and is reprinted with the permission of its publisher.
http://metmagazine.com/lessonplan/teaching_dynamics/

Grade Level:	Grades 5–6
Teacher's Technical Ability:	Intermediate
Objective:	Here is a basic lesson plan to introduce the concept of dynamics to students.
Materials/Equipment:	• Electronic instruments
	• "For You and Me" lead sheet (see "Download from www.ti-me.org/TIEMC").
	• "For You and Me" accompaniment (see "Download from www.ti-me.org/TIEMC").
	• Examples of statement/echo patterns for teaching dynamics (see "Download from www.ti-me.org/TIEMC").
	• "For You and Me" with dynamics (see "Download from www.ti-me.org/TIEMC").
Duration:	30–45 minutes (one class period)
How Electronic Keyboards Produce Dynamics:	Most electronic keyboards are velocity-sensitive, meaning that they respond to the speed, or velocity, with which each key is struck. When you strike a key, the keyboard generates a MIDI Note On message indicating that a specific note has been triggered. The Note On message also includes a velocity value that can range from 0 (no sound) to 127. For example, when you play a middle C with moderate speed, the keyboard generates a MIDI Note On message for note number 60 (middle C) with a velocity value of approximately 64. In most cases, higher velocity values produce louder, brighter sounds.
	Be aware that some low-cost electronic keyboards are not velocity-sensitive and cannot provide dynamic variation through keyboard performance.

Prior Knowledge and Skills: The students will need to know how to select different sounds on an electronic keyboard.

For You and Me

Fig. 1.9: "For You and Me" by Don Muro. This piece is to be played with General MIDI program 72 (clarinet) using the MP3 accompaniment provided on the TI:ME website.

Procedure:

1. First, ask your students to select General MIDI (GM) synthesizer program 72 (clarinet) and play the music (see "For_You_and_Me_No_Dynamics.pdf" on the TI:ME website and Fig. 1.9) using the accompaniment (see "For_You_and_Me_Accompaniment.mp3" also found on the TI:ME website).
   a. If there are two students at a keyboard, one student should play the part as written, and the other should play the part one octave higher.

2. When they are finished playing, ask the students if they heard any changes in the accompaniment.

3. If they are unable to identify the dynamic changes, play the accompaniment again and ask the students to listen without playing.

4. Lead their responses until they can define "dynamics" as the degree of loudness or softness in music.

5. Next, demonstrate the concept of dynamics by playing loud and soft sounds on classroom instruments such as piano, guitar, and Orff instruments.
   a. Be sure to demonstrate obvious sudden changes in dynamics.
   b. If no classroom instruments are available, use recordings of solo acoustic instruments or play imitative sounds on your electronic keyboard.

6. Get students thinking by asking the following questions:
   a. How do you control dynamics on a piano? (Answer: by striking the keys with varying amounts of force.)
   b. How do you control dynamics on a trumpet? (Answer: by increasing or decreasing the amount of air pressure.)
   c. How do you control dynamics on a violin? (Answer: by increasing or decreasing the amount of pressure from the bow.)
   d. Practically speaking, controlling dynamics on an electronic keyboard works much as it does with an acoustic piano: when the keys are struck quickly, the dynamic level is loud; when the keys are struck slowly, the dynamic level is soft. The difference is "under the hood," and most students will not know that part unless you explain it (see "How Electronic Keyboards Produce Dynamics" above).

7. Ask your students to experiment with the velocity sensitivity on different sounds.
   a. Although all GM synthesizer sounds respond to MIDI Velocity messages, sounds such as GM 9 (celesta) and GM 11 (music box) have a relatively narrow dynamic range that may be less apparent to the students.

8. Next, ask the students to select sound GM 66 (alto sax) and to echo the two-measure phrases you will play.

9. Begin by playing simple one-note patterns with one change in dynamics, and then gradually add more notes and dynamic changes to the two-measure patterns (see "Statement_Echo_Dynamics.pdf" on the TI:ME website).

    a. If students do not have individual speakers at their stations, have them raise their hands and let them play their echo patterns for the class through the lab headsets.

10. Next, introduce students to dynamic markings and their meanings, beginning with *pp* and ending with *ff*. Ask your students to look at the music ("For_You_and_Me_With_Dynamics.pdf") and to identify the dynamic markings that have been added to the score.

11. Invite them to perform "For You and Me" with the accompaniment using GM 76 (tenor sax), this time applying the new dynamic markings.

Evaluation: The students will perform "For You and Me" with appropriate dynamics on the electronic keyboard, using GM sound 76 (tenor saxophone).

Follow-up: Students should understand and recognize the importance of dynamics in most styles of music. Reinforce this concept by playing recorded examples of sudden dynamic changes in pieces such as the first movement of Beethoven's *Symphony No. 5* or Haydn's *Surprise Symphony*. If there are band or orchestra students in your class, ask them to bring their instruments and show how dynamics are controlled. Compare the different dynamic ranges of different acoustic instruments.

For homework, ask the students to find a recording that has no dynamic range, as well as a recording that has a wide dynamic range. The first part of the assignment will be easy; the second part will be far more difficult for some students but is well worth the effort.

Download from www.ti-me.org/TIEMC:
- "For_You_and_Me_No_Dynamics.pdf"
- "For_You_and_Me_With_Dynamics.pdf"
- "For_You_and_Me_Accompaniment.mp3"
- "Statement_Echo_Dynamics.pdf"

MENC Standards:	1. Singing, alone and with others, a varied repertoire of music.
	2. Performing on instruments, alone and with others, a varied repertoire of music.
	4. Composing and arranging music within specified guidelines.
	5. Reading and notating music.
	7. Evaluating music and music performances.
TI:ME Technology Areas:	1. Electronic instruments

"Old MacDonald Had a Band"
By Eileen Wolpert
Ancillae Assumpta Academy, Wyncote, Pennsylvania

Grade Level:	Grades 1–6
Teacher's Technical Ability:	Novice
Objective:	1. Students will play "Old MacDonald" on keyboards either in its entirety or just parts of the song.
	2. Students must use correct pitches and rhythms.
	3. Students will navigate the keyboard to find instruments belonging to one specific family.
	4. Students will use the song "Old MacDonald Had a Band" to perform their findings.

Materials/Equipment: A copy of the notation for "Old MacDonald." The file "Old_MacDonald.pdf" can be found on the TI:ME website (see "Download from www.ti-me.org/TIEMC" and Fig. 1.10).

Duration: 30 minutes

Prior Knowledge and Skills: Students are familiar with the piano keyboard—at least the notes F, G, and A.

Procedure:
1. Make sure all students are familiar with the placement of A, G, and F on the keyboard. Review if necessary.
2. Each student will play: AA GG F (e-i e-i o).

Old MacDonald Had a Band

Traditional

Old Mac-Don-ald had a farm;   E - I - E - I - O   And on his farm he

had   a   cow,   E - I - E - I - O   With a "moo - moo" here and a

"moo - moo" there   Here a "moo" there a "moo"   Ev-'ry-where a "moo - moo"

Old   Mac - Don - ald   had   a   farm,   E - I - E - I - O.

Old MacDonald had a farm, E-I-E-I-O
And on his farm he had a pig, E-I-E-I-O
With a (snort) here and a (snort) there
Here a (snort), there a (snort)
Everywhere a (snort, snort)
With a "moo-moo" here and a "moo-moo" there
Here a "moo", there a "moo"
Everywhere a "moo-moo"
Old MacDonald had a farm, E-I-E-I-O.

Old MacDonald had a farm, E-I-E-I-O
And on his farm he had a horse, E-I-E-I-O
With a "neigh" here and a "neigh" there
Here a "neigh", there a "neigh"
Everywhere a "neigh-neigh"
With a (snort) here and a (snort) there
Here a (snort), there a (snort)
Everywhere a (snort-snort)
With a "moo-moo" here and a "moo-moo" there
Here a "moo", there a "moo"
Everywhere a "moo-moo"
Old MacDonald had a farm, E-I-E-I-O.

Fig. 1.10: "Old MacDonald Had a Band."

19

3. The teacher or other more advanced piano students will play the song. All of the students will play AA GG F when appropriate in the piece:
   a. Old MacDonald had a band, *AAGGF*,
      And in his band he had a [*name of instrument*], *AAGGF*.
      With an *FF* here and an *FF* there,
      Here an *F*, there an *F*, ev'rywhere an *FF*.
      Old MacDonald had a band, *AAGGF*.
4. Use a particular family of instruments—winds (oboe, flute, clarinet, saxophone, bassoon).
5. One student can sing the song with the chosen instrument name inserted where needed while another student plays the sound of the chosen instrument with the correct pitches and rhythm in the appropriate places.
6. Ask the class:
   a. Was a wind instrument named in the song?
   b. Was the instrument's sound heard in the song?
   c. Were the correct pitches played with the correct rhythms?

Evaluation: Students will be able to play the sound of a given instrument with the correct pitches and rhythms to accompany "Old MacDonald."

Follow-up: Have students arrange other pieces of music using other instrumental timbres.

Items to Be Purchased: Electronic keyboards are required for this lesson.

Download from www.ti-me.org/TIEMC: "Old_MacDonald.pdf"

MENC Standards:	2. Performing on instruments, alone and with others, a varied repertoire of music.
	3. Improvising melodies, variations, and accompaniments.
	6. Listening to, analyzing, and describing music.
	7. Evaluating music and music performances.
TI:ME Technology Areas:	1. Electronic instruments

Making a Poem Come Alive with Sound

By Amy M. Burns
Far Hills Country Day School, Far Hills, New Jersey

Grade Level: K–5

Teacher's Technical Ability: Novice

Objective: The students will be able to successfully choose a sound on an electronic keyboard to enhance a poem.

Materials/Equipment:
- Electronic keyboards, preferably one per student; however it can be done with each keyboard shared between two students.
- Any poem that lends itself to be enhanced by sound. For this lesson, we use "Five Little Pumpkins," a traditional poem in the public domain.

Duration: 20 minutes

Prior Knowledge and Skills: The students should know how to change and experiment with sounds on the electronic keyboards. In addition, they should have read or sung the poem and experimented with classroom instruments before the lesson.

Procedure:
1. Before using this lesson with electronic keyboards, have the students first experiment on the poem with classroom instruments.
2. When the students arrive at the next class session, have them sit down and listen to the poem again. Alternatively, have a student volunteer to read the poem.
3. Assign each student a sound portrayed in the poem that he or she can eventually attempt to imitate it on the electronic keyboard. For example, in "Five Little Pumpkins":

Five little pumpkins sitting on a gate.
The first one said, "Oh my, it's getting late."
The second one said, "There are witches in the air."
The third one said, "Well, we don't care."
The fourth one said, "Let's run and run and run."
The fifth one said, "We're ready for some fun."
Whoooo–oooo went the wind, and out went the light.
And the five little pumpkins rolled out of sight!

The teacher can assign a student to be the wind sound; that student then has to find a sound on the electronic keyboard to that sounds like the wind. In addition, the teacher can assign a student to create a sound for the lights going out and other students to create sounds for the pumpkins.

4. Read the poem again, or have a student volunteer read the poem; now incorporate the electronic keyboards' sounds to enhance the poem.
5. Compare and contrast how the poem sounded with no instruments, classroom instruments, and finally, the electronic keyboards.

Evaluation: Since this lesson can produce various levels of achievement, the following rubric has been made to clarify assessment:

	Programming the electronic keyboard	Choosing an appropriate sound on the electronic keyboard to imitate the sound in the poem
Excellent	The student can program the keyboard with no assistance from the teacher.	The student can choose an appropriate sound to imitate the sound in the poem and explain why he/she chose that sound, with no assistance from the teacher.
Good	The student can program the keyboard with little assistance from the teacher.	The student can choose an appropriate sound to imitate the sound in the poem and explain why he/she chose that sound, with little assistance from the teacher.
Fair	The student can program the keyboard only with assistance from the teacher.	The student can choose an appropriate sound to imitate the sound in the poem and explain why he/she chose that sound, only with assistance from the teacher.
Novice	The student cannot program the keyboard even with assistance from the teacher.	The student cannot choose an appropriate sound to imitate the sound in the poem and cannot explain why he/she chose that sound, even with assistance from the teacher.

Follow-up: This lesson can be followed up with a combination of electronic keyboards and classroom instruments enhancing the sounds of the poem. (This is also ideal if the teacher does not have one electronic keyboard per student.) The students could again compare and contrast what they heard. Furthermore, if the class size is big, some students can be assigned to create movements to act out the poem while others are creating sounds to enhance the poem.

Items to Be Purchased: Electronic keyboards are required for this lesson. Since electronic keyboards can consume a small budget, the teacher should order one or two electronic keyboards per year. These keyboards need not to be expensive, just serve the purpose of the current music curriculum.

Download from www.ti-me.org/TIEMC: None

MENC Standards:
2. Performing on instruments, alone and with others, a varied repertoire of music.
3. Improvising melodies, variations, and accompaniments.
8. Understanding relationships between music, the other arts, and disciplines outside the arts.

TI:ME Technology Areas:
1. Electronic instruments

Elementary Students Improvising a Melody to "Baté Baté"

By Amy M. Burns
Far Hills Country Day School, Far Hills, New Jersey

Grade Level: Grades 2–4

Teacher's Technical Ability: Novice

Objective: The students will improvise a melody to the rhythm of the words from the traditional Mexican chant, "Baté Baté," on the black keys of a keyboard.

Materials/Equipment:
- Traditional chant of "Baté Baté" (see Fig. 1.11 and "Download from www.ti-me.org/TIEMC").
- Rhythm patterns used in the chant.
- Classroom instruments.
- Any type of electronic keyboards.

Duration: 30 minutes

Prior Knowledge and Skills: The students need to be able to identify and perform quarter- and eighth-note patterns. The students should be familiar with a keyboard.

Procedure:
1. Introduce the traditional Mexican chant "Baté Baté." I usually write the chant with the rhythms on the classroom easel (see Fig. 1.11).
2. At the second through fourth grade levels, students are able to read the rhythms fairly well. However, if they are having trouble reading the rhythm patterns, then they will echo me to learn the chant.
3. Clap and perform the chant.
4. Once they are secure with the chant, add classroom instruments to play the rhythm of the words.

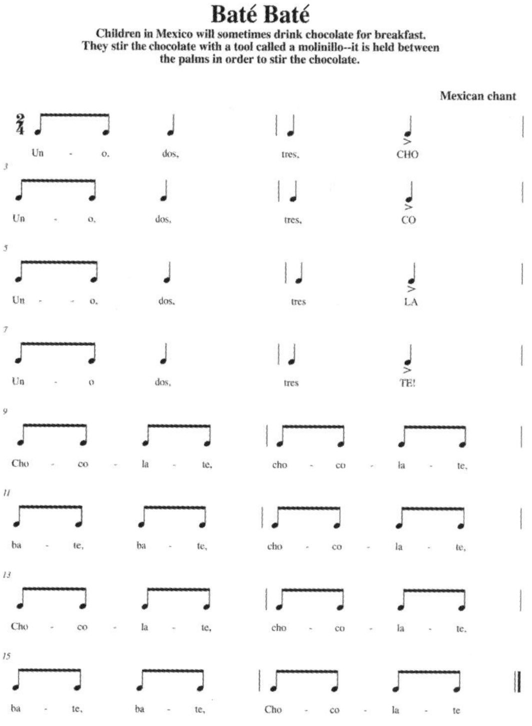
Baté Baté
Children in Mexico will sometimes drink chocolate for breakfast. They stir the chocolate with a tool called a molinillo--it is held between the palms in order to stir the chocolate.
Mexican chant
Un - o, dos, tres, CHO
Un - o, dos, tres, CO
Un - o, dos, tres LA
Un - o dos, tres TE!
Cho - co - la - te, cho - co - la - te,
ba - te, ba - te, cho - co - la - te,
Cho - co - la - te, cho - co - la - te,
ba - te, ba - te, Cho - co - la - te

Fig. 1.11: "Baté Baté."

5. Then have the students go to the keyboards, which are preset to GM sound 14—marimba. Play an alternating low G♭ and low D♭ to the steady beat on your keyboard, then demonstrate how to improvise on the black keys to the rhythm of the words.

6. The students should improvise a melody together using the black keys of the keyboard while you play the steady beat on the alternating low G♭ and low D♭. Since the black keys form a pentatonic scale, all of their improvised melodies playing together sound good.
   a. If you do not have enough keyboards for each student to play individually, then this lesson would work fine if you double the students up, two per keyboard.
   b. If you have a limited number of keyboards, then you can have the students take turns between Orff instruments, classroom instruments, and keyboards.

7. When they can improvise the chant securely on the black keys of the keyboard, have them choose different sounds to perform their improvisations. When you do this, it would be beneficial to have earphones for the students so they do not disturb each other when choosing their sounds.

Evaluation: I evaluate younger students on the accuracy of their rhythms and older ones on their keyboard technique (*i.e.*, finger position, playing on only the black keys as opposed to pressing some white keys, and so on) in addition to rhythmic accuracy.

Follow-up: For the next lesson, review how to improvise "Baté Baté" and record the students' improvisations on digital audio software, such as Apple's GarageBand or Cakewalk Sonar Home Studio.

Items to Be Purchased: This lesson requires electronic keyboards. Since electronic keyboards can consume a small budget, the teacher should order one or two electronic keyboards per year. These keyboards need not to be expensive, just serve the purpose of the current music curriculum.

Download from www.ti-me.org/TIEMC: "Bate_Bate.pdf"

MENC Standards:	2. Performing on instruments, alone and with others, a varied repertoire of music.
	3. Improvising melodies, variations, and accompaniments.
	6. Listening to, analyzing, and describing music.
	7. Evaluating music and music performances.
TI:ME Technology Areas:	2. Music production

Improvising Third and Fourth Graders

By Amy M. Burns
Far Hills Country Day School, Far Hills, New Jersey

Grade Level:	Grades 3–4
Teacher's Technical Ability:	Novice
Objective:	To improvise a two-measure question and a two-measure answer using the notes B, A, and G above middle C on the recorder.
Materials/Equipment:	• Recorders.
	• Auto accompaniment software such as PG Music's Band-in-a-Box or a looping program where you can create a looping accompaniment such as Apple's GarageBand or Sony's Acid Music Studio. For this lesson, we will use Band-in-a-Box.
	• There is an example of an accompaniment on the TI:ME website (see "Download from www.ti-me.org/TIEMC").
	• "Au Clair de la Lune" (see Fig. 1.12, which can also be found on the TI:ME website).
Duration:	30 minutes
Prior Knowledge and Skills:	The students can identify, read, finger, and perform the notes B, A, and G above middle C on the recorder.

Soprano Recorder

Au Clair de la Lune

Traditional

Fig. 1.12: "Au Clair de la Lune."

Procedure:

1. Review the notes B, A, and G above middle C with the students. You can do this through various songs, methods, and/or drills. An example of a song that uses these three notes is the traditional French song "Au Clair de la Lune."

2. Once you have reviewed the three notes, have the students create a four-note (quarter notes) answer to your four-note question. For example, you play a four-note melody using the notes B, A, and G, and make your last note A or B so the melody sounds like a "question." Then, the students will "answer" you by playing a four-note melody using the same notes (B, A, G) and ending on the note G.

3. Continue improvising, but this time play a two-measure "question" using quarter and half notes ending on B or A, and they respond with a two-measure answer using quarter and half notes and ending on the note G.

4. Compare and contrast how "Au Clair de la Lune" has a two-measure "question" and a two-measure "answer."

5. Now play an accompaniment you created in Band-in-a-Box, so that the students can perform a two-measure "answer" to your two-measure "question."
   a. If you use Band-in-a-Box, you could choose a style like "Heavy Rock" (my students love this style). Click on "S" and scroll down to "Heavy Rock."
   b. Type the letter "G" in the first measure. On the second half of the second measure, type the letter "D." Then type the letter "G" in the third measure. To finish the accompaniment, click on the number 3 ("Number of Choruses in the Song") and scroll to the desired number of choruses that you want the students to play, in this case 1. Then click on the number 32 ("Chorus End Bar") and click on "measure four," so that the accompaniment will end on measure four.
   c. In Band-in-a-Box, the song will begin again unless you press "Stop." This is a nice feature because you can have the students improvise numerous times. You could also have the song play more than one chorus, as stated in 5b.
   d. If you do not want to create the song, but would like the Band-in-a-Box file, see the MIDI file in "Files on the Website."

6. Once students are comfortable improvising as a group, have them improvise the answer individually as you improvise the question.

7. Switch and have the students improvise the question (remind them to end on A or B) and you improvise the answer.

8. After they complete this successfully, have the students divide into groups of two and improvise questions and answers with each other.

Evaluation: The following rubric was created so that you can accurately assess the students as a whole or in groups of two. However, you might not feel that this would be ideal in your situation. Therefore, please feel free to adapt this rubric to fit your needs.

	The group can improvise a two-measure answer on the notes B, A, and G using quarter and half notes when the teacher improvises a two-measure question.	**The students can improvise a two-measure question and a two-measure answer when working in pairs, using the notes B, A, and G with the rhythms of quarter and half notes.**
Excellent	90–100 percent of the group can improvise a two-measure answer on the notes B, A, and G using quarter and half notes when the teacher improvises a two-measure question.	Both students can improvise a two-measure question and a two-measure answer using the notes B, A, and G with the rhythms of quarter and half notes with no assistance from the teacher.

Good	75–89 percent of the group can improvise a two-measure answer on the notes B, A, and G using quarter and half notes when the teacher improvises a two-measure question.	Both students can improvise a two-measure question and a two-measure answer using the notes B, A, and G with the rhythms of quarter and half notes with little assistance from the teacher.
Fair	50–74 percent of the group can improvise a two-measure answer on the notes B, A, and G using quarter and half notes when the teacher improvises a two-measure question.	Only one student in the group of two can improvise a two-measure question and a two-measure answer using the notes B, A, and G with the rhythms of quarter and half notes. The other student can only do this with much assistance from the teacher.
Novice	0–49 percent of the group can improvise a two-measure answer on the notes B, A, and G using quarter and half notes when the teacher improvises a two-measure question.	Neither of the two students can improvise a two-measure question and a two-measure answer using the notes B, A, and G with the rhythms of quarter and half notes even with much assistance from the teacher.

Follow-up: The next lesson would involve improvising a four-measure question with a four-measure answer. As the students progress on the recorder (or Orff instrument) and learn more rhythms and notes, you can expand the improvisations to include the new notes and rhythms.

Items to Be Purchased: This lesson uses PG Music's Band-in-a-Box (http://www.pgmusic.com), an inexpensive creative, practice, and performance software.

Download from www.ti-me.org/TIEMC:
- "Au_Clair_de_la_Lune.pdf"
- "Improvising_3rd_4th_grade.mp3"
- "Improvising_3rd_4th_grade.MID"

MENC Standards:	1. Singing, alone and with others, a varied repertoire of music.
	2. Performing on instruments, alone and with others, a varied repertoire of music.
	3. Improvising melodies, variations, and accompaniments.
	4. Composing and arranging music within specified guidelines.
	5. Reading and notating music.
	6. Listening to, analyzing, and describing music.
	7. Evaluating music and musical performances.
	8. Understanding relationships between music, the other arts, and disciplines outside the arts.
	9. Understanding music in relation to history and culture.
TI:ME Technology Areas:	1. Electronic instruments
	2. Music production
	3. Notation software
	5. Multimedia

The Music of Wild Birds:
Melody Structure, Improvisation, and Recording
By Matthew Etherington
Camelot Academy, Durham, North Carolina
http://www.music4education.com/resources/birdsong

Grade Level:	Grades 3–6
Teacher's Technical Ability:	Intermediate
Objective:	Students will improvise melodies in response to wild birdcalls. Students will analyze melody structures including pitch, rhythm, tempo, and ornamentation. Students will record an improvised melody with either Apple's GarageBand or Audacity. Students will reflect on and assess their own and each other's improvised melodies. Students will relate listening and performing experiences to written musical symbols.
Materials/Equipment:	This lesson is to be performed in a keyboard lab with computers. It can also be adapted for performance with recorders and one computer hooked up to a screen or TV. Other items that are required:

- Website: http://www.music4education.com/resources/birdsong/.
- Book: *Fieldbook of Wild Birds and Their Music* by F. Schuyler Mathews (Applewood Books, 2001, ISBN: 1557095183).
- Either MIDI keyboards with Apple computer(s) and GarageBand, or soprano recorders with PC computer(s) and Audacity.

Duration:	45 minutes
Prior Knowledge and Skills:	The students will need to have either basic GarageBand skills (recording an audio track) or the ability to record an audio track in Audacity, and basic soprano recorder fingerings if you're not using keyboards.
Procedure:	1. Play a selection of bird songs from the website in class. For web address, see "Materials."
	2. Using notation on the board, ask students to guess which pattern fits which audio example.
	3. Students explore the website on their computers with headphones and experiment with melody ideas on the keyboard/recorder.
	4. Ask students to choose one of the bird songs and improvise a melody based on the pitch, rhythm, tempo, and ornamentation of the example.
	5. Students record their melody into GarageBand or Audacity.
	6. Students play their recordings to each other and appraise their own and each other's melodies.
Evaluation:	The student evaluates his/her own improvisation upon playback of the recording. The class evaluates the recording of the student's melody. The teacher assesses the recorded melody for pitch, rhythm, tempo, and ornamentation at a later time.
Follow-up:	Students should notate their melodies with a graphic score, or traditional notation. Students can perform songs about birds, such as "Yellow Bird" and "Three Little Birds."
Items to Be Purchased:	1. Apple's GarageBand comes automatically installed on all new Mac computers. If you have a Mac computer but do not have GarageBand, you can order it from http://www.apple.com/ilife/garageband/ for the educator's price. You can also use the freeware Audacity http://audacity.sourceforge.net/) on either a Mac or PC.
	2. Electronic keyboards (optional because you can use soprano recorders).
	3. Soprano recorders (if not using keyboards).
	4. Audacity: a freeware sound editing software program that can be used on a Mac or PC and can be downloaded at http://audacity.sourceforge.net/
	5. Headphones for electronic instruments (optional)
	If you do not have access to a keyboard or a computer lab, but you do have a computer in your classroom room and your students perform on recorders, then you just need to hook the computer to a screen or TV and download Audacity. This means that this lesson can be done for free.
Download from www.ti-me.org/TIEMC:	None

MENC Standards:	2. Performing on instruments, alone and with others, a varied repertoire of music.
	3. Improvising melodies, variations, and accompaniments.
TI:ME Technology Areas:	1. Electronic instruments
	2. Music production

12-Bar Blues Accompaniment

By Dr. Thomas E. Rudolph
Haverford School District, Haverford, Pennsylvania

This article was previously published in the December 2003 issue of *Music Education Technology* magazine,
a property of Penton Media, and is reprinted with the permission of its publisher.
http://metmagazine.com/lessonplan/new_accompanist

Grade Level:	Grades 5–6
Teacher's Technical Ability:	Intermediate
Objective:	The students will improvise a melody using a 12-bar blues progression and PG Music's Band-in-a-Box software.
Materials/Equipment:	• PG Music's Band-in-a-Box program. To create a song using Band-in-a-Box, simply type in the chords using the computer keyboard. Once the chord symbols are entered, the next step is to select a style, such as jazz, rock, bossa nova, waltz, or classical. The program also offers many other styles.
	After entering the chords and selecting the style, press the "Play" button and Band-in-a-Box will instantly generate piano, bass, and drum accompaniment parts. Then record a melody, or the program can generate one. Accompaniment software programs also let you transpose a song to any key and adjust the tempo. Save the resulting files to disk and reuse them later.
Duration:	30 minutes
Prior Knowledge and Skills:	I usually begin the composition process with my students using tonic, dominant, and subdominant harmony. After students have listened to various compositions using these harmonic elements, they can create their own pieces using auto-accompaniment software.

Procedure: One of my favorite lessons is to introduce several songs that use a 12-bar blues progression. I usually begin with a familiar 12-bar blues progression such as "In the Mood." I write the chord progression for the class and ask the class to analyze the blues progression while keeping the following questions in mind:

1. What are the first and last chords? Answer: The tonic.
2. What is the most frequently used chord? Answer: The tonic.
3. What three chords are used in the 12-bar blues progression? Answer: The tonic (I), dominant (V), and subdominant (IV).

I then ask the students to compose their own version of the 12-bar blues, following these three rules. After entering their original chord progression, students can select from one of the styles, adjust the tempo, and improvise a melody on the MIDI keyboard.

Evaluation: The students will compose their own 12-bar blues song and improvise a melody using a MIDI keyboard.

Follow-up: Students can enter chords from an existing tune or create their own chord progressions. Other activities include harmonizing a melody and improvising over chord symbols.

Items to Be Purchased: PG Music's Band-in-a-Box (http://www.pgmusic.com)—an inexpensive software that combines basic notation, accompaniment, and MIDI programs in one—and its competitors make terrific composition tools because they instantly play back chord progressions. It is worth considering adding Band-in-a-Box to your budget because it serves so many purposes of the music curriculum.

Download from
www.ti-me.org/TIEMC:
- "12_Bar_Blues_Bb.mp3"
- "12_Bar_Blues_C.mp3"

MENC Standards: 1. Singing, alone and with others, a varied repertoire of music.

TI:ME Technology Areas: 2. Music production

Assessing Your Young Students' Voices

By Amy M. Burns
Far Hills Country Day School, Far Hills, New Jersey

Grade Level: K–2

Teacher's Technical Ability: Intermediate

Objective: The teacher will be able to use music technology to help assess whether his/her students are singing in tune.

When I read the MENC General Music bulletin boards, a concern that continuously appears is how to assess young children for the purpose of grading. This is even more difficult if you see 400 students per week. This lesson addresses one way to accurately assess each student.

Materials/Equipment:
- Apple iPod that has recording capabilities—the previous iPod photo (fourth generation iPod) or the current video or classic iPod.
- External recording device, such as XtremeMac MicroMemo voice recorder (see Fig. 1.13). Please note that the MicroMemo is a separate purchase from the iPod.

—or—

- M-Audio's MicroTrack (see Fig. 1.14), a professional two-channel mobile digital recorder. The MicroTrack comes with its own microphone, so there is no need to purchase an additional microphone.

Fig. 1.13: XtremeMac MicroMemo.

In order to assess the students accurately, you will need to sit them in an assigned seating order. Choose a song that the students can sing into the recording device. For this lesson, I will use the traditional Halloween song "Skin and Bones" to assess if the students can sing the line "Ooh-ooh-ooh-ooh" (mi-re-do-la) for this lesson. Please note that this is a song that I would use in my classroom. You can choose to use a song that best fits your curriculum.

Fig. 1.14: M-Audio's MicroTrack.

Duration: 30 minutes (one class period)

| Prior Knowledge and Skills: | The objective of this lesson is for the teacher to assess the students' singing abilities. Therefore, the students need to be able to sing a song that they know well. |

Procedure:

1. Review singing the song together as a group.
2. Sing the line "Ooh-ooh-ooh-ooh" together with the hand symbols for mi-re-do-la.
3. Create movements to reinforce the melodic direction of the line "Ooh-ooh-ooh-ooh."
4. Explain to the students that you will be recording the line "Ooh-ooh-ooh-ooh" as each student takes turns singing it solo.
5. Demonstrate how to sing the line into the voice recorder. Press "Record," then hand it to the first student. If you have concerns with your students holding the recording device, you can place it in the middle of room to record the students.
6. Have all students sing the verses together, with each one taking a turn singing the line "Ooh-ooh-ooh-ooh" into the voice recorder.
7. When finished, you will have a recording of each student singing a solo line of the song.

Evaluation:

Now that you have a recording with each of your students singing a solo, you can listen to it from the iPod by connecting it to a set of speakers, or you can import it onto your computer and listen to it from there. Depending on your goals for your students, you can assess them on what best fits your curriculum. For this lesson, I have assessed them with the following rubric:

	Singing the line "Ooh-ooh-ooh-ooh" on the correct pitches of mi-re-do-la.
Excellent	The student can sing all of the proper pitches of mi-re-do-la in tune.
Good	The student can sing 3 out of 4 proper pitches of mi-re-do-la in tune.
Fair	The student can sing 1–2 out of 4 proper pitches of mi-re-do-la in tune.
Novice	The student cannot sing any of the proper pitches of mi-re-do-la in tune.

Follow-up:

This assessment is a way for you to assess many students, especially for report cards.

Items to Be Purchased:

The price of Apple's iPod varies depending on how many gigabytes (GB) you want. Please note that teachers qualify for educators' discounts, so please check Apple's web-site at http://www.apple.com for these discounts. The XtremeMac MicroMemo micro-phone (http://www.xtrememac.com/audio/ earphones_recorders/micromemo.php) for the iPod is relatively inexpensive. M-Audio's MicroTrack is costly if you have a tight music budget; however, it does come with its own microphone and can be used to record performances, podcasts, music projects, etc. M-Audio's MicroTrack can be found at http://www.m-audio.com.

Download from www.ti-me.org/TIEMC: None

MENC Standards: 1. Singing, alone and with others, a varied repertoire of music.
7. Evaluating music and musical performances.

TI:ME Technology Areas: 2. Music production

Preparing Your General Music Classes for a Concert: Part 1

By Amy M. Burns
Far Hills Country Day School, Far Hills, New Jersey

Grade Level: K–6

Teacher's Technical Ability: Intermediate

Objective: To prepare your elementary general music classes for a concert.

When I read the MENC General Music bulletin boards, one item that often appears is how to keep the students' attention spans focused on concert preparation when they are singing the same songs every class period. The following two lessons ("Preparing Your General Music Classes for a Concert: Part 1" and "Preparing Your General Music Classes for a Concert: Part 2") will give you ideas on how to keep your students focused on the upcoming concert, as well as assessing them in unique ways with the assistance of technology.

Materials/Equipment:
- Concert music that you have chosen.
- Assessment rubric (optional—see "Download from www.ti-me.org/TIEMC")
- Recording device. This recording device could be one of the following:

Fig. 1.15: XtremeMac MicroMemo.

A computer that has digital audio software. This could range from the freeware Audacity to a professional audio/MIDI software such as MOTU's Digital Performer. Most computers have built-in microphones that would suffice for recording purposes. However, if you need a more professional microphone, the Shure (http://www.shure.com) line of microphones has several excellent microphones that are relatively inexpensive.

Apple's iPod with the XtremeMac MicroMemo voice recorder (see Fig. 1.15).

M-Audio's MicroTrack, a professional two-channel mobile digital recorder (see Fig. 1.16).

Fig. 1.16: M-Audio's MicroTrack.

Duration:	One to two music classes

**Prior Knowledge
and Skills:** The students will need to have learned their concert music before you record them.

Procedure:
1. Review the lyrics of the concert song with the students.
2. Explain to the students that you will be recording them as they sing their songs so that they can hear themselves later.
3. To record the song:
   a. If you are using Audacity, just launch the software and press the red "Record" button, after which you will see the bar start to move across the screen and the sound waves appear as the students begin to sing. To end the recording, just press the yellow square "Stop" button.
   b. If you are using the iPod with the MicroMemo voice recorder attached, just press the center button on the iPod twice. This will make the iPod record. To end the recording, just press the "Pause" button and click "Stop and Save."
   c. To record on the MicroTrack, make sure that the microphone is attached and press the "Record" button. To end the recording, just press the "Record" button again.
4. To hear the recording of your students played back:
   a. If you are using Audacity, just scroll back to the beginning by pressing the left arrow, then press the green "Play" button. If the computer's volume is too soft, you can just turn it up. If the volume is still too soft, you can always purchase a pair of speakers, which range from the inexpensive computer speakers you find at Staples, to the more expensive, professional speakers that you find at any music retailer.
   b. To hear the playback with an iPod, save the recording, then connect the iPod to external speakers (like those mentioned above), or connect your iPod to its dock that contains speakers.
   c. If you are using the MicroTrack, you can connect it to external speakers (like those mentioned above).
5. You can use this recording in the following ways:
   a. You can play the recording back to them so that they can listen to their own singing. The students will love to hear themselves singing together.
   b. You can ask the students to listen to the recording to assess themselves about breathing, phrasing, enunciation, etc.
   c. You can listen to the recording later in order to assess the class on pitch accuracy, memorization (do they know all of the lyrics?), phrasing, enunciation, articulation, rhythm, etc.

Evaluation: I have put an assessment rubric here (see Fig. 1.17) and on the TI:ME website. However, you can make your own rubric based on whatever musical concept you are evaluating.

Follow-up: If your students are singing rounds, please see the follow-up lesson "Preparing Your General Music Classes for a Concert: Part 2." In addition, based on either your assessment or the students' assessment of themselves, you can plan your next class accordingly.

ASSESSMENT RUBRIC

When listening to the recording, circle the answer that best applies.

1. Could you understand the words that the students were singing?
   a. EXCELLENT – Most of the time.
   b. GOOD – Some of the time.
   c. FAIR – Rarely.
   d. NOVICE – Not at all.

2. How were the students' phrases?
   a. EXCELLENT – They breathed in all of the correct places and held out words to the proper rhythms.
   b. GOOD – They breathed in most of the correct places and held out words to the proper rhythms some of the time.
   c. FAIR – They breathed, sometimes in the correct places, sometimes not. They rarely held out words.
   d. NOVICE – When they breathed, they broke one word into two and they could not hold out words when they were supposed to.

3. Do the students have the lyrics memorized?
   a. YES – The students did not need any prompting from the teacher.
   b. FOR THE MOST PART – The students needed very little prompting from the teacher.
   c. SOMETIMES – The students needed plenty of prompting from the teacher.
   d. NOT YET – The teacher's singing voice can be heard for most of the song.

4. How is the class's pitch in general?
   a. EXCELLENT – Most of the time, the pitch is accurate.
   b. GOOD – Some of the time the pitch is accurate. In addition, some of the time, the students have the correct intervals; however, they are beginning on the wrong pitch.
   c. FAIR – Rarely, the pitch is accurate and some students are chanting.
   d. NOVICE – The students have become too excited and are now shouting the song.

Fig 1.17: Assessment rubric.

Items to Be Purchased: This lesson can be done with a computer and the freeware Audacity (http://audacity.sourceforge.net/). If you have a laptop or computer with Internet access and download the freeware, then this will cost you nothing. However, be aware that audio files take up a significant amount of space on a computer's hard drive. If you purchase the M-Audio's MicroTrack (http://www.m-audio.com), or Apple's iPod (http://www.apple.com) with the XtremeMac MicroMemo (http://www.xtrememac.com/audio/earphones_recorders/micromemo.php), then this will run you a few hundred dollars.

Download from www.ti-me.org/TIEMC: "Concert_Rubric_Part_One.pdf"

Preparing Your General Music Classes for a Concert: Part 2

By Amy M. Burns
Far Hills Country Day School, Far Hills, New Jersey

Grade Level:	K–6
Teacher's Technical Ability:	Intermediate
Objective:	To prepare your elementary general music classes for a concert that involves a round, partner song, or a song featuring two-part harmony.
Materials/Equipment:	When I read the MENC General Music bulletin boards, one item that often appears is how to keep the students' attention spans focused on concert preparation when they are singing the same songs every class period. The following two lessons ("Preparing Your General Music Classes for a Concert: Part 1" and "Preparing Your General Music Classes for a Concert: Part 2") will give you ideas on how to keep your students focused on the upcoming concert, as well as assessing them in unique ways with the assistance of technology.

- Concert music that you have chosen.
- Recording device. This recording device could be one of the following:
  A computer that has digital audio software. This could range from the freeware Audacity to a professional audio/MIDI software such as MOTU's Digital Performer. Most computers have built-in microphones that would suffice for recording purposes. However, if you need a more professional microphone, the Shure (http://www.shure.com) line of microphones has several excellent microphones that are relatively inexpensive.

Fig. 1.18: XtremeMac MicroMemo.

Apple's iPod with the XtremeMac MicroMemo voice recorder (see Fig. 1.18).

M-Audio's MicroTrack, a professional two-channel mobile digital recorder (see Fig. 1.19).

Fig 1.19: M-Audio's MicroTrack.

Duration: One to two music classes

Prior Knowledge and Skills: The students will need to have learned their concert music before you record them.

Procedure:
1. Review the round, partner song, or a song that features two-part harmony.
2. Explain to the students that you will be recording them so that the other class that sings the other part of the round, partner song, or song with two-part harmony will be able to practice along with the recording.
3. The advantages of this are:
   a. If you do not have an accompaniment CD that provides the other part, then the recording will assist the students in practicing with the other part.
   b. Though I think that CD accompaniments featuring both parts are a good way for the students to practice, many times these CDs have not been of much assistance. This is because the voices on the CD are wonderfully professional while my students sound like the elementary general music class that they are (some sing off pitch; some chant the music; some sing with a light tone, some with a heavy tone; some are silent as they stare at the audience, etc.). Therefore, having the students practice along with the others whom they will actually perform with provides better results than if they were to practice with an accompaniment CD.
4. To record the song:
   a. If you are using Audacity, just launch the software and press the red "Record" button. As the students begin to sing, the bar will then start moving across the screen and the sound waves will appear. To end the recording, just press the yellow square "Stop" button.
   b. If you are using the iPod with the MicroMemo voice recorder attached, just press the center button on the iPod twice. This will make the iPod record. To end the recording, just press the "Pause" button and click "Stop and Save."
   c. To record on the MicroTrack, make sure that the microphone is attached and press the "Record" button. To end the recording, just press the "Record" button again.
5. To hear the recording of your students played back:
   a. If you are using Audacity, just scroll back to the beginning by pressing the left arrow, then press the green "Play" button. If the computer's volume is too soft, just turn it up. If the volume is still too soft, you can always purchase a pair of speakers, which range from the inexpensive computer speakers you find at Staples, to the more expensive, professional speakers that you find at any music retailer.
   b. To hear the playback with an iPod, first save the recording, then connect the iPod to external speakers (like those mentioned above), or to its dock that contains speakers.
   c. If you are using the MicroTrack, you can connect it to external speakers (like those mentioned above).
6. When you have recorded both parts of the round, partner song, or song that features two-part harmony, play back the recording so that the students can practice along with the other part.

Evaluation: As the students practice with the other recorded part, evaluate whether they are having trouble singing their own part while the other part is playing.

Follow-up: If they are having problems singing their own part while the other part is playing, have them rehearse until they seem comfortable.

Items to Be Purchased: This lesson can be done with a computer and the freeware Audacity (http://audacity.sourceforge.net/). If you have a laptop or computer with Internet access and download the freeware, then this will cost you nothing. However, be aware that audio files take up a significant amount of space on a computer's hard drive. If you purchase M-Audio's MicroTrack (http://www.m-audio.com), or Apple's iPod (http://www.apple.com) with the XtremeMac MicroMemo (http://www .xtrememac.com/audio/ earphones_recorders/micromemo.php), then this will run you a few hundred dollars.

Download from www.ti-me.org/TIEMC: None

PART 2

TECHNOLOGY-ENHANCED LESSON PLANS THAT EMPHASIZE NOTE READING AND CREATING AND COMPOSING MUSIC BY ADDRESSING THE MENC STANDARDS 4 AND 5:

4. **Composing and arranging music within specified guidelines.**
5. **Reading and notating music.**

Creating Music within a Specified Form

By Amy M. Burns
Far Hills Country Day School, Far Hills, New Jersey

Grade Level:	K–2
Teacher's Technical Ability:	Novice
Objective:	The students will create a song within the specified guidelines to the form: A-B-A-C-A-D-A-E-A.

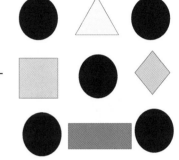

Fig. 2.1: The form of Vivaldi's "Spring" (A-B-A-C-A-D-A-E-A) represented by shapes and colors.

Materials/Equipment:

- Audio recording of Antonio Vivaldi's "Spring" from *Four Seasons*, Op. 8, Movement 1.
- Listening chart that visually represents the form A-B-A-C-A-D-A-E-A (see Fig. 2.1).
- Computer with speakers, projected onto a TV or screen, or a Smart Board. This projection requires an adapter that runs from your computer into the screen.
- Sibelius's Groovy Music. For this lesson, we will use Groovy Shapes from the Groovy Music series.

Duration: 30 minutes

Prior Knowledge and Skills: This lesson is a part of a unit on form. Before this lesson, the students would have identified the form of Vivaldi's "Spring," from *The Four Seasons*, Op. 8, Movement 1. They would have listened to the song while following the listening chart and moving to the form of the piece.

Procedure:

1. Create an "A" section in Groovy Shapes by selecting loops (see Fig. 2.2) before the lesson.
2. When the students enter the room, Groovy Shapes is open and present on the TV screen.
3. When the students are settled, review the form of Vivaldi's "Spring" Movement 1—A-B-A-C-A-D-A-E-A— through movement.
4. Inform the students that together they are going to create their own song using the same form.

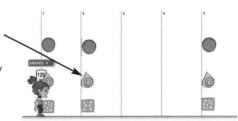

Fig. 2.2: The arrow is pointing at the "A" section created in Sibelius Groovy Music Shapes.

5. Students gather around the TV that has the Groovy Shapes "A" section projected onto the screen.

6. Show the students Groovy Shapes. Play the A section that you created before class by pressing the "Play" button. The students will see the main character walk across the screen. When the A section is being played, the character will be walking under the shapes that represent certain sound loops (see Fig. 2.3). For sections B, C, D, and E, the character will walk under a blank screen and nothing will sound.

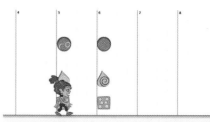

Fig. 2.3: When the song plays, a character of your choosing will walk or leap across the screen. The blank measures are for the B, C, D, and E sections.

7. Ask the students what they thought of the song. Most common responses will be that they liked it and that the drums sounded cool, but they did not like the silent parts.

8. Explain that the students will help you create the music for B, C, D, and E sections using Groovy Shapes.

9. Present the students with some boundaries when creating the sections so that they feel successful when making the song. For example, offer to them choices, such as: "For the B section, we can choose between this drum shape and sound, or that drum shape and sound; now we can choose between this guitar shape and sound or that guitar shape and sound." This helps eliminate indecision and/or hurt feelings among the students because of too many choices.

Evaluation: The students as a group will successfully identify and create a song with the form A-B-A-C-A-D-A-E-A, using Sibelius's Groovy Shapes.

Follow-up: This lesson can be followed up by having the students listen to their song in Groovy Shapes and analyzing it by identifying what instruments they heard, melodic direction, and which sections they liked the best and the least. In addition, if you have the funds to purchase the lab pack, you can have the students break into small groups and create another song using a different form.

Items to Be Purchased: If you have a computer in your classroom or on your cart, then the only additional items that need to be purchased are the software, Sibelius's Groovy Shapes (http://www.sibelius.com/products/groovy/index.html), and speakers to amplify the sound from the computer. Sibelius's Groovy Shapes is a relatively inexpensive, easy-to-use software. It is well worth the price. You might also need to purchase an adapter that will project your computer screen onto a TV. However, check with your school because an adapter may be a part of the school's inventory. The only extra step you might want to consider is to sign out the TV, projection screen, or Smart Board in advance.

Download from www.ti-me.org/TIEMC: None

MENC Standards:	4. Composing and arranging music within specified guidelines.
TI:ME Technology Areas:	4. Instructional music software

A "Groovy" Haiku:
Enhancing a Haiku with Sibelius's Groovy Jungle
By Amy M. Burns
Far Hills Country Day School, Far Hills, New Jersey

Grade Level:	Grades 2–6
Teacher's Technical Ability:	Novice
Objective:	The students will write a poem and orchestrate sounds within specified guidelines to enhance the haiku. In addition, this lesson can also correspond with poems that are written in the classroom.
Materials/Equipment:	• Sibelius' Groovy Jungle from the Groovy Music Series. • Computer. • CD of *Carnival of the Animals.*

In this lesson, the students will write a haiku. I have done this lesson in coordination with a study of Camille Saint-Saëns's *Carnival of the Animals.* Hence the need for the CD. This can also be done in coordination with a poetry unit done in class. However, I will present this lesson as a part of a unit study of Saint-Saëns's *Carnival of the Animals.*

Here is one example of a third grader's haiku about the swan:
The swan is pretty.
It moves with grace and beauty
on top of water.

Duration:	30 minutes
Prior Knowledge and Skills:	The students will have listened to Camille Saint-Saëns's *Carnival of the Animals.* In addition, they will have studied the instruments and themes that correspond with the animals and movements. Furthermore, they understand how to write a haiku—a 17-syllable verse form consisting of three metrical units of 5, 7, and 5 syllables, and know how to use Sibelius's Groovy Jungle software.
Procedure:	1. Assign each student to write a haiku, based on the animals of Camille Saint-Saëns's piece, *Carnival of the Animals.* a. If you have access to a computer lab, have the students write the poem during the first music class, then orchestrate the poem while using Sibelius's Groovy Jungle in the second music class, which would occur in the computer lab.

b. If you do not have access to a computer lab, you can have the class use one computer that is projected onto a Smart Board, TV, or screen. So that each student gets a turn on the computer, divide your class into groups. Assign one of the animals from *Carnival of the Animals* to each group. The group will then write haikus about their animals. When they are finished, they will orchestrate their haiku using Groovy Jungle, taking turns with the one computer in the classroom.

2. Have each student type the haiku into Groovy Jungle by logging in, pressing the "Create" button, and then pressing the "A" button on screen. Once the students have done this, they can type in their haiku.

3. After their haiku are entered, ask the students to choose a melody (represented by butterflies), a bass line (bushes), and a chord (spider web). To reinforce Saint-Saëns's orchestration, have them change the melody's instrumentation to Saint-Saëns's instrumentation. For example, if the student is composing a melody for the swan, I will have the student change the instrument to the cello. This can easily be done by clicking on the rainbow wheel, then clicking and dragging the cello to the melody line (butterfly) that was placed on the screen.

Fig 2.4. Finished Haiku using Groovy Jungle.

4. Remind the students to listen to their compositions carefully to see how the music they chose corresponds with the words of their haiku.

5. If there is time, encourage your students to choose dynamics and tempos to enhance the words of their haiku.

6. When finished, have them save their haiku.

7. To see a finished product, please see Fig. 2.4.

Evaluation: Depending on how you choose to use this lesson, there are a variety of outcomes. If the students are composing their haiku in their classrooms, then you are evaluating them on how they compose music within your specified guidelines. If the students are composing their haiku in your music room based on a work such as Saint-Saëns's *Carnival of the Animals*, then you are also evaluating them on how well they write a haiku using the three metrical units of 5-7-5.

Follow-up: During the next class, have each student share his/her haiku with the class. Have the student recite the haiku alone, then have him/her recite it with the orchestration that he/she created with Groovy Jungle.

Items to Be Purchased: The items used in this lesson are Sibelius's Groovy Jungle (http://www.sibelius.com/ products/groovy/index.html), a computer, and speakers to amplify the composition. Groovy Jungle is inexpensive and can be purchased as a single copy or in five-user lab packs.

Download from www.ti-me.org/TIEMC: None

| **MENC Standards:** | 5. Reading and notating music. |
| **TI:ME Technology Areas:** | 3. Notation software |

Oops, I Did It Again
By Susan J. Nichols
Amherst Middle School, Amherst, New Hampshire

Grade Level:	Grades 2–6
Teacher's Technical Ability:	Novice
Objective:	The objective of the lesson is for the students to be able to correctly identify musical notation on the staff.
Materials/Equipment:	Create a worksheet full of various kinds of errors in manuscript writing (missing clef, oversized notes, stems too long and/or backwards or missing, too many/not enough beats per measure, etc.). To see a sample of this worksheet, please see "Download from www.ti-me.org/TIEMC."
Duration:	40–45 minutes
Prior Knowledge and Skills:	Knowledge of the treble clef and the treble clef notes is helpful. Basic rhythms (whole notes through eighth notes) should already be understood in order to use the downloadable worksheet. Otherwise, you may customize according to your students' abilities. Students will have a very basic knowledge of what written music looks like without the skills of writing a manuscript correctly.
Procedure:	1. The worksheet is the "hook." It is full of errors in printing/writing music.
	2. To begin the lesson, students should identify as many of the errors as possible.
	a. Elementary students can be very competitive: "I wonder who will find the most errors on this worksheet!"
	3. Each student has his/her own sheet to work on and circles the "misteaks" with a pencil. He/she then lists the mistakes at the bottom of the page.
	4. When students are finished, a teacher-facilitated discussion ensues with students identifying the errors.
	5. At each error point, the teacher can teach the correct method (for adding stems, for sizing notes, etc.).
Evaluation:	The worksheet and discussion will reveal the level of understanding. A sequential activity would be for the students to write the same composition on manuscript paper with all errors omitted. Teacher may collect one or both to measure understanding.
Follow-up:	If the goal of manuscript writing is for students to accurately write compositions (outside of the benefits of a computer lab), then the students can proofread their own as well as a partner's composition to check for similar errors.

Items to Be Purchased: This lesson can be done manually, without the assistance of music notation software. However, students will respond better to worksheets made with notation software because the worksheets look neater, are easier to read, and save time to make. A notation program, such as Finale or Sibelius, will work for this lesson plan. These notation programs can be fairly inexpensive or costly depending if you are a novice or expert user of this software.

Finale: http://www.finalemusic.com/

Sibelius: http://www.sibelius.com/products/sibelius/index.html

Download from
www.ti-me.org/TIEMC:

- "Oops!_Find_the_Mistakes.pdf"
- "Oops!_Find_the_Mistakes.mus"—created in Finale and can be adapted in Finale or Sibelius if needed.

MENC Standards:	5. Reading and notating music.
TI:ME Technology Areas:	4. Instructional music software (computer-assisted instruction, or CAI)
	5. Multimedia

Can You Spell These Words?
A Note-Naming Game Using the Classics for Kids Website
By Amy M. Burns
Far Hills Country Day School, Far Hills, New Jersey

Grade Level:	Grades 2–5
Teacher's Technical Ability:	Novice
Objective:	The objective of this lesson is to have the students spell the musical words on the treble clef staff, using only the notes found on the lines and spaces of this staff. Therefore, this game does not involve notes on the ledger lines.
Materials/Equipment:	• A large staff.
	• Notes to place on the staff.
	• A computer.
	• The website http://www.classicsforkids.com.
	• A TV, Smart Board, or LCD projector so that the students can see the website.
	• Assessment rubric (see "Download from www.ti-me.org/TIEMC").
Duration:	20–30 minutes
Prior Knowledge and Skills:	The students need to know the note names on a treble clef staff.
Procedure:	1. Review the note names of a treble clef staff:

      a. Take out a large staff (this could be a felt staff, a staff drawn on an easel, a staff used as a carpet, etc.).

      b. Review lines and spaces.

      c. Review the note names on the staff with the method that you taught the students to identify and comprehend the note names on a treble clef staff.

    2. Play the game:

      a. Before you begin, please go over good sportsmanship if you decide to play a game that divides the class into two teams. In my school, I have an excellent P.E. program, so when I speak about sportsmanship to the students, they have already experienced it in their P.E. classes and know how to practice it.

      b. Connect your computer to a TV, Smart Board, or LCD projector.

      c. Launch the Classics for Kids website (http://www.classicsforkids.com).

      d. Click on "Games."

      e. Click on the "Note Name Game" (see Fig. 2.5).

f. The game will appear with the notes dancing from side-to-side on the staff. They dance from side-to-side until you place the correct letters beneath them.

g. Divide the class into two teams. I usually name my two teams after composers, such as "Team Bach" and "Team Beethoven."

Fig. 2.5: Classics for Kids Note Name Game.

h. The first few words that appear on the screen are only three-letter words. As the students progress, the words have more letters.

i. Assign Team Bach to go first.

j. The goal is to drag the correct letter name to the space below each note to spell a word.

k. For a three-letter word, such as "EGG" (see Fig. 2.5), have three members of the Bach team go to the computer (or Smart Board) and drag the letter to the corresponding note. When the student puts the correct letter under the note, he/she earns Team Bach a point. Therefore, for the word "EGG," if all three students place the correct letters under the notes, then Team Bach has earned three points. If a student does not place the letter under the correct note, the computer gives you a sound to let you know that the letter was incorrect and the team does not earn a point. I will usually give each student two tries to earn the point.

l. The game will give you ten words to spell. Many times, the team that earns the most points is the one who had the words with the most letters. Therefore, at the end I give each student (on both teams) a reward of a musical pencil or a lollipop. It is up to you to decide if and how to reward them.

Evaluation: As the students each take a turn, sit in the back of the classroom and evaluate each student individually on their ability to name notes. If you choose, you can also evaluate each student for sportsmanship. The following is a rubric designed to assess each student at naming notes. You can easily print this rubric from the TI:ME Website.

	Assessing students at naming notes
Excellent	The student can successfully name the note on the treble clef staff on the first try with no assistance from the teacher.
Good	The student can successfully name the note on the treble clef staff on the second try with no assistance from the teacher.
Fair	The student can successfully name the note on the treble clef staff on the second try with assistance from the teacher.
Novice	After two attempts, the student is not yet ready to successfully name the note on the treble clef staff.

Follow-up: This lesson can be followed up with more note-naming games like "Musical Hangman"—a game in which only words comprised of the seven letters of the musical alphabet are used—or the creating of compositions with the notes of a treble clef staff.

Items to Be Purchased: If you have one computer with Internet access in your classroom and you are able to hook it up to a TV, LCD projector, or a Smart Board, then you do not need to purchase any additional items for this lesson.

Download from www.ti-me.org/TIEMC: Assessment rubric titled "Can_You_Spell_These_Words.pdf"

MENC Standards:	4. Composing and arranging music within specified guidelines.
	6. Listening to, analyzing, and describing music.
	7. Evaluating music and musical performances.
TI:ME Technology Areas:	4. Instructional music software
	5. Multimedia

Reinforcing Crescendo and Decrescendo with Sibelius's Groovy Jungle

By Amy M. Burns
Far Hills Country Day School, Far Hills, New Jersey

Grade Level: Grades 1–3

Teacher's Technical Ability: Novice

Objective: The students will be able to identify and compose with the dynamics symbols of fortissimo *ff*, forte *f*, piano *p*, pianissimo *pp*, crescendo, and decrescendo.

Materials/Equipment:
- Sibelius's Groovy Jungle.
- Computer hooked to a TV, LCD projector, or Smart Board.
- Optional: For older students, these two lessons can be performed in a computer lab.

Duration: Two 30-minute classes

Prior Knowledge and Skills: I utilize these two lessons when I am teaching and reinforcing to the students the concept of dynamics.

Procedure: **Class 1: Review and reinforce dynamic symbols**
1. Review the concepts of "loud" and "soft" through singing, playing instruments, and performing movement activities.
2. Reinforce the concepts of dynamics using Groovy Jungle lesson 4, "Dynamics Symbols."
   a. Hook your computer to a TV, LCD projector, or Smart Board. For this example, we will use the TV.
   b. Have the students sit around the TV.
   c. Launch Groovy Jungle, create a character, press "Explore," then press "Dynamics Symbols."
   d. If you need to adjust the volume or any other settings in Groovy Jungle, press "Shift+Control+T" (for either Mac or PC).
3. Have the students complete the lesson together by choosing various students to go to the computer and complete each activity.

4. The students will identify and comprehend dynamic symbols such as of fortissimo *ff*, forte *f*, piano *p*, pianissimo *pp*, crescendo ◁, and decrescendo ▷ (see Fig. 2.6a, b, and c).

Did You Know?

Did you know that if you hold down the Shift and Control keys (both Mac and PC) and press on the letter of the lesson, you can move to that lesson without having to complete the preceding lessons?

Class 2: Create music with Groovy Jungle utilizing dynamic symbols

1. Before class 2, I create a four-measure "A" section in Groovy Jungle that has a bass line (trees) and a melody (butterflies). The song will have an ABA form, where the students will create the "B" section.
2. Launch Groovy Jungle and press "Create."
3. When the students enter, have them sit around the TV; play the "A" section for them.
4. Inform the students that they will be creating the "B" section and that they will experiment with dynamics to see how it affects the song.
5. Have the students use arpeggios (bees) and chords (spider webs) to create the "B" section.
6. Once they agree that they like the "B" section, have them assign dynamics to each section. This is done by pressing the rainbow circle at the bottom left-hand corner of the screen (see Fig. 2.7).
7. My students decided to make the "A" sections *f* (forte) and the "B" section *p* (piano). In addition, they chose to decrescendo into the "B" section and crescendo back into the "A" section. You can see most of the song in Fig. 2.8.

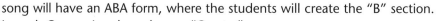

p cresce**ndO** *f*

p ◁ *f*

Fig. 2.6 a, b, and c: Sequential progression of learning dynamic symbols in Groovy Jungle.

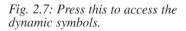

Fig. 2.7: Press this to access the dynamic symbols.

Fig. 2.8: The ABA (portion of the returning "A" section is cut off) song.

8. For a close-up of the dynamics, see Figs. 2.9a and b.

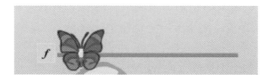 

Fig. 2.9a and b: To place a dynamic symbol in Groovy Jungle, just click and drag the symbol to the melody, or bass line, or chord, etc.

9. Have the students listen to the song and ask them how the dynamics affected the song. Depending on the age group, a young group might answer that it made the song sound "cool" or "good." An older group will comment that they could hear the sections better because the dynamics were different for each section.

Evaluation: Since Groovy Jungle is being used to assist the teacher in reinforcing the concept of dynamics and dynamic symbols, you will be able to evaluate their comprehension and progress through observation.

Follow-up: This lesson can be followed up with another lesson in which students either sing or play instruments on very simple songs. As you hold up the dynamic symbols on cards, the students must perform the songs according to the symbol.

Items to Be Purchased: Sibelius's Groovy Jungle (http://www.sibelius.com) is an inexpensive software that can be purchased as a single copy, as a lab pack, or as a site license.

Download from www.ti-me.org/TIEMC: None

MENC Standards:	4. Composing and arranging music within specified guidelines.
	5. Reading and notating music.
TI:ME Technology Areas:	3. Notation software

Introducing Notation Software: Part 1
Preparations and Dragging Notes

By Dr. Thomas E. Rudolph
Haverford School District, Haverford, Pennsylvania

This article was previously published in the November 2006 issue of *Music Education Technology* magazine,
a property of Penton Media, and is reprinted with the permission of its publisher.
http://metmagazine.com/lessonplan/introducing_notation_software

Grade Level:	Grades 3–6
Teacher's Technical Ability:	Intermediate
Objective:	The students will be able to identify, sing, arrange, and perform the notes and pitches for the song "Hot Cross Buns" in the key of C.
Materials/Equipment:	• Almost any music-notation program, such as Avid Technology Sibelius (www.sibelius.com), MakeMusic Finale (http://www.codamusic.com) or Finale Notepad (http://www.codamusic.com/notepad/default.aspx), VirtuosoWorks Notion (http://www.notionmusic.com/), Adept Nightingale (http://www.ngale.com/), NoteHeads Igor Engraver (http://www.noteheads.com/), and GenieSoft Overture (http://www.geniesoft.biz).
	• Notation files for "Hot Cross Buns," which can be found on the TI:ME website (see "Download from www.ti-me.org/TIEMC").
Duration:	20 minutes
Prior Knowledge and Skills:	This approach is successful with students at any level, so long as they are able to read basic notation, use a mouse to drag pitches, and learn to click on notes using the mouse or a MIDI keyboard.
Procedure:	1. When arranging exercises and guiding students in composition, it helps to create a file for them in which they can manipulate notes, rather than asking them to starting entering notes from scratch. I provide students with instructions, and they open the prepared file on their computers. They then enter their changes, save their file, and print it out.
	2. To prepare a file for your students, select a song that most students already know, such as a folk song. Before attempting this activity, students should be able to sing or play the song. I often use songs such as "Lightly Row," "Hot Cross Buns," and "Twinkle, Twinkle, Little Star."

3. Next, create a notation file and enter the rhythm of the melody but with all of the notes set to the starting pitch (see Fig. 2.10). Instruct the students to create the correct melody by clicking and dragging the notes to the correct staff locations, starting with the second pitch (see "Download from www.ti-me.org/TIEMC").

Hot Cross Buns

Click the mouse on the note head and drag them to the correct location

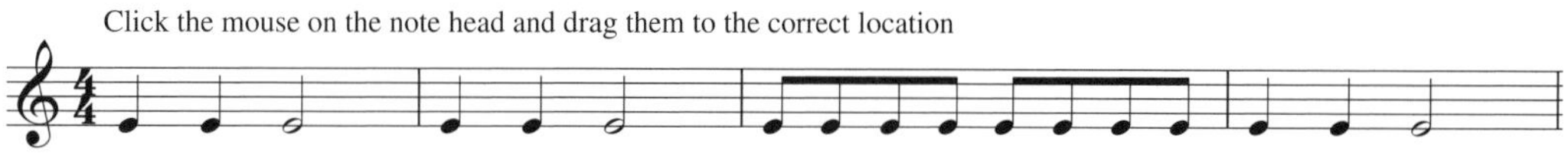

Fig. 2.10: This "Hot_Cross_Buns_Same_Notes" file can be found on the TI:ME website.

4. This is a good ear-training exercise, and it helps students get used to moving and editing pitches in a notation program. Since you have prepared the file in advance, you do not have to spend class time teaching your students how to create a new score. That can come later.
5. Once your students become comfortable with dragging existing notes, create a second example. This time, leave some measures in the score totally blank (see Fig. 2.11).
6. Instruct the students on how to enter notes into a score by using the mouse, typing on the computer keyboard, and playing a MIDI keyboard.

Hot Cross Buns

Complete the missing notes

Fig. 2.11: In this example, some measures are left blank so that students can enter the missing notes.

7. Have the students save the files, or do it yourself.

Evaluation: The teacher will evaluate the students on how well they arrange the notes to form the correct melody of "Hot Cross Buns."

Follow-up: See the next lesson titled, "Introducing Notation Software: Part 2—Adding Lyrics and Chords."

In addition, the note-dragging concept can be extended to more-advanced lessons. For instance, create a file of a Bach chorale or some other four-part harmony example. Assign all of the pitches to the starting pitch of each voice and ask your students to drag the pitches to the correct locations. You will need to play the piece for them on the keyboard or provide an audio file. You can also have students create a melody by dragging notes to accompany a chord progression, such as the 12-bar blues. There are 12-bar blues accompaniments on the TI:ME website labeled as "12_Bar_Blues_Bb.mp3" or "12_Bar_Blues_C.mp3."

Download from www.ti-me.org/TIEMC:
- "Hot_Cross_Buns_Intro_Same_Notes.mus"
- "Hot_Cross_Buns_Intro_Same_Notes.sib"
- "Hot_Cross_Buns_Intro_Same_Notes.mid"
- "Hot_Cross_Buns_Intro_Missing_Notes.mus"
- "Hot_Cross_Buns_Intro_Missing_Notes.sib"
- "Hot_Cross_Buns_Intro_Missing_Notes.mid"

| MENC Standards: | 4. Composing and arranging music within specified guidelines. |
| | 5. Reading and notating music. |

| TI:ME Technology Areas: | 3. Notation software |

Introducing Notation Software: Part 2
Adding Lyrics and Chords

By Dr. Thomas E. Rudolph

Haverford School District, Haverford, Pennsylvania

This article was previously published in the November 2006 issue of *Music Education Technology* magazine,
a property of Penton Media, and is reprinted with the permission of its publisher.
http://metmagazine.com/lessonplan/introducing_notation_software

Grade Level:	Grades 3–6
Teacher's Technical Ability:	Intermediate
Objective:	The students will be able to identify and compose the lyrics and chord symbols for the song, "Hot Cross Buns," in the key of C.
Materials/Equipment:	• Almost any music-notation program, such as Avid Technology Sibelius (www.sibelius.com), MakeMusic Finale (http://www.codamusic.com) or Finale Notepad (http://www.codamusic.com/notepad/default.aspx), VirtuosoWorks Notion (http://www.notionmusic.com/), Adept Nightingale (http://www.ngale.com/), NoteHeads Igor Engraver (http://www.noteheads.com/), and GenieSoft Overture (http://www.geniesoft.biz).
	• "Hot Cross Buns" notation file created in part 1, which has the correct melody.
Duration:	20 minutes
Prior Knowledge and Skills:	This approach is successful with students at any level, so long as they are able to read basic notation, use a mouse to drag pitches, and learn to click on notes using the mouse or a MIDI keyboard.
Procedure:	1. Open the file the students created for "Hot Cross Buns." They will need the file they created in part 1 that has the correct melody.
	2. Ask the students to enter the lyrics for the song.
	3. With the lyrics in place, have them add the chord symbols. In this manner, the students learn how to create a lead sheet.
	4. Students who play an instrument can be taught how to transpose the melody for a B♭, an E♭, or some other transposing instrument.

5. If your notation software has plug-ins that allow enhancements, such as adding a drum groove, let your students experiment.

6. In a classroom or lab setting, play the students' completed assignments for the entire class. Ask the rest of the class to sing the roots of the chords and identify the chord progressions.

Evaluation: The teacher will evaluate the students on how well they add lyrics and chord symbols to "Hot Cross Buns."

Follow-up: As with all activities, some students will complete the initial exercises quickly and others will take longer. Have those who are done first add a percussion part to their piece. By adding a percussion staff and assigning it to MIDI channel 10 (find out how your notation software handles percussion staves), students can add rhythmic accompaniments to melodies (see Fig. 2.12).

Hot Cross Buns

Fig. 2.12: Adding a percussion staff and assigning it to MIDI channel 10 enables students to create rhythmic accompaniments.

You can also ask your students to create a harmony part to accompany the melody. If your students have very little background in music theory, instruct them to experiment with thirds and sixths, and to include contrary motion whenever possible.

After students master the beginning stages of note entry, they can be led into creating entire melodies and harmonies from scratch. Variations of the note-dragging approach can be offered with more complex songs throughout the semester or course.

Download from www.ti-me.org/TIEMC: None

55

MENC Standards:	2. Performing on instruments, alone and with others, a varied repertoire of music.
	4. Composing and arranging music within specified guidelines.
	5. Reading and notating music.
	6. Listening to, analyzing, and describing music.
	7. Evaluating music and musical performances.
TI:ME Technology Areas:	3. Notation software

Composer B-A-G Variations
By Carol Childers

Grade Level:	Grades 3–6
Teacher's Technical Ability:	Novice–Intermediate
Objective:	Students will vary a melody using the following compositional techniques: retrograde, augmentation, diminution.
Materials/Equipment:	• Computer.
	• Recorders.
	• Overhead projector.
	• Overhead transparency with "Hot Cross Bun" and blank measures (see "Download from www.ti-me.org/TIEMC").
	• Notation software. See "Download from www.ti-me.org/TIEMC" for ready-to-use files formatted for Finale (.mus), Sibelius (.sib), or any music notation program (.mid).
Duration:	30 minutes

Prior Knowledge and Skills:

1. Melodic notation B-A-G.
2. Basic rhythmic notation.
3. Beginning recorder skills.
4. B-A-G melody that was composed in past lesson.

Procedure:

1. On an overhead projector, show the melody for "Hot Cross Buns" (see Fig. 2.13).
2. Explain retrograde.
3. Show blank measures on an overhead, and rewrite notes for "Hot Cross Buns" in retrograde.

Fig. 2.13: "Hot Cross Buns."

4. Explain augmentation.
5. On blank measures, rewrite notes for "Hot Cross Buns" in augmentation with notes becoming twice their original value.
6. Follow the same procedure for diminution only—notes become 1/2 of original value.
7. Using previous B-A-G composition students compose three variations: retrograde, augmentation, diminution.
8. Print variations and play them on the recorder.

Evaluation: The teacher grades the printed version of each variation.

Follow-up: Make a final composition by cutting and pasting from the original melody and its three variations. Compose a final composition in theme and variations. Discuss how the variations changed the sound of their melodies. Discuss how a composer might use these variation techniques in a song.

Items to Be Purchased: Notation software such as Sibelius (http://www.sibelius.com) or Finale (http://www.finalemusic.com).

Download from www.ti-me.org/TIEMC:
- "Hot_Cross_Buns.pdf"
- "Hot_Cross_Buns.mid" to be opened with any musical notation software. Most likely, you will need to type in the title of the composition depending on the software that you are using.
- "Hot_Cross_Buns.mus" can be opened using any version of the Finale software (http://www.finalemusic.com). It was created using Finale 2007.
- "Hot_Cross_Buns.sib" can be opened using any version of the Sibelius (http://www.sibelius.com) notation software. It was created using Sibelius 4.

MENC Standards:	1. Composing and arranging music within specified guidelines.
	5. Reading and notating music.
	6. Listening to, analyzing, and describing music.
TI:ME Technology Areas:	3. Notation software

Composing with Notation Software

By Dr. Thomas E. Rudolph

Haverford School District, Haverford, Pennsylvania

This article was previously published in the September 2003 issue of *Music Education Technology* magazine, a property of Penton Media, and is reprinted with the permission of its publisher.

http://metmagazine.com/mag/scoring_points/

Grade Level:	Grades 4–6
Teacher's Technical Ability:	Intermediate
Objective:	The students will learn how to enter a three-part round such as "Are You Sleeping?" using notation software, create an arrangement of instruments, and compose a percussion part.
Materials/Equipment:	I have found that the best way to proceed is for the teacher to create files before the start of class and copy them to the hard drive of each computer. This can usually be done over the school network. The students then open the file that you have created, and modify and add to it. This procedure decreases the skill level that students need in order to complete each exercise. This is especially important when dealing with a large class in a computer or MIDI lab.
Duration:	30–40 minutes
Prior Knowledge and Skills:	Use your notation software to create a four-staff score with three different instruments and one percussion staff. Enter the entire melody for "Are You Sleeping?" ("Frère Jacques") in the top staff. Include text to give the students the directions for the lesson (see Fig. 2.14).

Are You Sleeping?

Traditional

Fig. 2.14: The notation for "Are You Sleeping?" in the key of C major.

| Procedure: | I usually write these instructions at the top of the page of the file that I create. |

1. "Are You Sleeping?" ("Frère Jacques"):
2. Enter the second and third parts of the round either by clicking in the notation using the mouse or by copying and pasting.

3. After the three-part round is completed, experiment with different instrument timbres for the various parts. Change the instrument timbres and volumes of each part.
4. Compose a percussion part on the fourth staff using quarter- and eighth-note patterns.
5. Play the results back often and make changes to your arrangement.
6. Save and then print the composition.

Evaluation: The students share with each other their round with the added percussion part. The other students listen and analyze each composition.

Follow-up: For additional exercises, make variations on the format we have just discussed. You can create a file and have your students complete the assignment. The key to developing notation lessons is to have a specific goal for students to accomplish and to provide them with a partially completed file.

Items to Be Purchased: The ideas presented can be used with any such program, including Sibelius Software's Sibelius (http://www.sibelius.com); Finale Music's Finale, PrintMusic, and NotePad (http://www.finalemusic.com); and a variety of others. You can purchase a site license for a notation program such as PrintMusic or Sibelius. If budget is a big concern, consider using Finale Music's free notation program, NotePad, which can be downloaded from the company's website.

Download from www.ti-me.org/TIEMC:
- "Are_You_Sleeping.sib" can be opened using any version of the Sibelius notation software. It was created using Sibelius 4.
- "Are_You_Sleeping.mus" can be opened using any version of the Finale software. It was created using Finale 2007.
- "Are_You_Sleeping.mid" can be opened with any musical notation software. Most likely, you will need to type in the title of the composition depending on the software that you are using.

Several books, websites, and tips can help you develop more lessons using notation software:
- *Teaching Music with Technology* by Tom Rudolph (GIA Publications, 2nd edition, 2004). There is a chapter on notation and several lessons on the book's accompanying CD.
- *Technology Strategies for Music Education* (TI:ME, 2002). TI:ME's book includes more than 200 strategies for integrating technology into the curriculum.
- Vermont MIDI Project (http://www.vtmidi.org). Here you will find a wealth of student work using notation software. For example, look at sample student compositions; the descriptions of how the students were asked to compose their music can provide many ideas for your students' projects.

MENC Standards:	4. Composing and arranging music within specified guidelines.
	5. Reading and notating music.
TI:ME Technology Areas:	4. Instructional music software (computer-assisted instruction, or CAI)

Naming Notes and Composing a Question-and-Answer Melody

By Anna Anderson
Woodward Elementary School, Massachusetts

Grade Level:	Grades 2–4
Teacher's Technical Ability:	Novice
Objective:	1. Students will review note names and placement on staff.
	2. Students will compose simple question-and-answer using Doodle Pad in Harmonic Vision's Music Ace 1 or Music Ace Maestro software.
Materials/Equipment:	• Computer connected to an LCD projector.
	• Worksheet with a story on it. Some words are spelled in treble clef notes (for examples of this worksheet, see "Download from www.ti-me.org/TIEMC").
	• Harmonic Vision's Music Ace 1, lessons 7 and 8 (or Music Ace Maestro lessons 8 and 10) and Doodle Pad.
	• Computer lab or multiple computers.
Duration:	3 class periods
Prior Knowledge and Skills:	1. Definitions and understanding of staff, pitch, and note names.
	2. Improvisations of short question-and-answer tunes with partners.
Procedure:	1. Students sing a song that the teacher normally sings at the beginning of class.
	2. Students echo/read a few rhythms on "du-de-du" and echo a few intervals after the teacher.
	3. The students sit around the LCD projector connected to a computer and review how to use Music Ace 1 (or Music Ace Maestro).
	4. Students will come up, each in turn, to complete lessons 7 and 8 (treble staff) of Music Ace 1 software program (or lessons 8 and 10 of Music Ace Maestro).
	5. Students will be divided into two teams to compete in the game portion of the lessons.
	6. Students will work on individual computer stations in the lab on their two-phrase question-and-answer composition using Doodle Pad found in Music Ace 1 or Music Ace Maestro.
	7. Students will fill out a review sheet that tells a story by decoding the words spelled with the notes in the treble clef (for examples of this worksheet, see "Download from www.ti-me.org/TIEMC").

Evaluation: 1. The teacher will conduct informal evaluations as students answer questions in the lesson.
2. The teacher will check the worksheet.
3. The teacher will check the composition and evaluate it for the understanding of question-and-answer phrasing.

Follow-up: 1. The composition can also be done with the question phrase composed with only high pitches and the answer phrase composed with only low pitches, and vice versa. That segues nicely into the first lesson on Music Ace software, high/low pitch (lesson 1 for Music Ace Maestro); and also the third lesson, playing with pitch (lesson 4 for Music Ace Maestro).
2. Doodle Pad has a nice feature in that the round notes equal longer rhythmic values (*i.e.*, half and whole notes) and the skinny notes equal shorter rhythmic values (*i.e.*, quarter and eighth notes). That can lead into a rhythmic value lesson.

Items to Be Purchased: This lesson requires Harmonic Vision's Music Ace Software (http://www .harmonicvision.com). Please check the website for prices and information on a single version, lab packs, network licenses, etc.

Download from
www.ti-me.org/TIEMC:
- "Note_Spelling_Game.pdf"
- "Note_Spelling_Game_Answer.pdf"
- "Note_Spelling_Game2.pdf"
- "Note_Spelling_Game2_Answer.pdf"

MENC Standards:	2. Performing on instruments, alone and with others, a varied repertoire of music.
	4. Composing and arranging music within specified guidelines.
	5. Reading and notating music.
	6. Listening to, analyzing and describing music.
	7. Evaluating music and music performances.

| TI:ME Technology Areas: | 1. Electronic instruments |
| | 2. Music production |

Podcasting with Elementary Students

By Amy M. Burns
Far Hills Country Day School, Far Hills, New Jersey

Grade Level: Grades 1–3

Teacher's Technical Ability: Intermediate

Objective: The students will tell the story of Sergei Prokofiev's *Peter and the Wolf* and will create their own sounds for each character of *Peter and the Wolf* using classroom percussion instruments, Orff instruments, or keyboards. The characters include Peter, Bird, Duck, Cat, Grandpa, Wolf, and Hunters. In addition, the teacher will record the students playing the characters' sounds and publish them as a podcast on the school's website or a free podcasting website.

Materials/Equipment:
- CD of Prokofiev's *Peter and the Wolf.*
- Pictures of the characters: Peter, Bird, Duck, Cat, Grandpa, Wolf, and Hunters (you can make your own or you can see "Download from www .ti-me.org/TIEMC" below).
- Rhythm patterns that the students will use to create the characters' sounds (see Fig. 2.15 and "Download from www.ti-me.org/TIEMC" below). Depending on the abilities of my students, I have had them create the rhythm patterns using quarter notes, eighth notes, half notes, and quarter rests.
- Classroom percussion instruments, Orff instruments, or keyboards.
- A computer that has digital audio software. This could range from the freeware Audacity (http://audacity.sourceforge.net/) to an inexpensive audio software such as Apple's GarageBand to a more professional audio/MIDI software such as MOTU's Digital Performer (http://www.motu.com). Most computers have built-in microphones that would suffice for recording purposes.

—or—

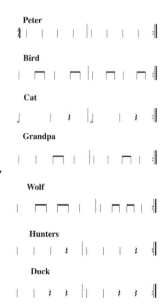

Fig. 2.15: Rhythm patterns for the characters of Prokofiev's Peter and the Wolf.

Apple's iPod (http://www.apple.com) with the XtremeMac MicroMemo (http://www.xtrememac.com/audio/earphones_recorders/micromemo.php) voice recorder

—or—

M-Audio's MicroTrack (http://www.m-audio.com), a professional two-channel mobile digital recorder

Duration: This lesson is one of the last lessons I use with my first graders when we study Prokofiev's *Peter and the Wolf*. Prior to this lesson we have listened to the story, drawn pictures representing the story line and the various characters, studied the orchestral instruments via listening examples and visiting the San Francisco Symphony website (http://www.sfskids.org), and acted out the story. I use this podcasting lesson to assess what the students have learned. It will take about two 30-minute class periods depending on the attention span of the students.

Prior Knowledge and Skills: Students should have prior knowledge of how to read and perform quarter notes, eighth notes, half notes, and quarter rests. In addition, they will have experienced *Peter and the Wolf* as stated above in "Duration."

Procedure:
1. Explain to the students that they will be recording their own *Peter and the Wolf* that their parents can listen to on a website.
2. Ask the students to tell you the story of *Peter and the Wolf* so you can narrate the story. If they are having any trouble retelling the story, help them by providing clues, such as "Was Grandpa happy that Peter went into the meadow?"
3. Once this is finished, divide the class into seven groups. Each group represents a character: Peter, Bird, Duck, Cat, Grandpa, Wolf, and Hunters.
4. Explain to the students that you will narrate the story as they have told it to you. In addition, when you speak about their group's character, they will use classroom instruments, or Orff instruments, or keyboards to represent that character.
5. Have all groups clap their characters' rhythm patterns. Work together to have the group achieve success when clapping the rhythm patterns.
6. Now have each group find an instrument to perform the rhythm pattern of the character.
7. Practice the story before you record it with the students. They will need various reminders about how to perform their rhythm patterns and when they are to play their instruments. If you use the character graphics from the TI:ME website, then the visualizations will help them with this.
8. Once the story is ready, press "Record" on your audio software such as Audacity, GarageBand, Digital Performer, or your audio recording device such as the iPod with the Micromemo or the MicroTrack.
9. Read the story and pause when the students are to perform their rhythm patterns for their characters.
10. Once finished, press the "Pause" or "Stop" button and save the file.
11. To publish the audio file on your school's website, you will need to check with your school's tech department or tech person to understand what the procedure is for loading an audio file to the website. Please note that this will be just an audio file that students and parents can access.
12. To publish the podcast on your own website:
    a. GarageBand and Apple's iWeb can easily be used. GarageBand has excellent loops and an easy-to-use process to save the podcast (if the website is created with iWeb). However, this works only on Macs.
    b. Use a software titled Tool Factory (http://www.toolfactory.com) It is an easy-to-use application for those with a PC who would like to begin podcasting.

13. If you do not have a website, but would like to publish a podcast, there is currently a website called podOmatic where users can create free podcasts. PodOmatic (http://www.podomatic.com) is a free, customizable podcast page that can hold up to 500MB of space per podcast. You will need to become a member to publish a podcast, however it is simple to do. If you would like to begin publishing your podcasts for assessment purposes or so that you can get your music curriculum more visible by your parents, then this is a nice and easy way to do it.

Evaluation: Since this lesson can produce a variety of outcomes, this rubric was created to help you assess your students (you can also find this rubric on the website):

	Students can read and perform their characters' rhythm patterns	Students can tell you the story of *Peter and the Wolf*
Excellent	90–100 percent of the students can perform the rhythm patterns with little or no assistance from the teacher.	The students tell the story of *Peter and the Wolf* accurately with no assistance from the teacher.
Good	70–89 percent of the students can perform the rhythm patterns with little or no assistance from the teacher.	The students tell the story of *Peter and the Wolf* accurately with little assistance from the teacher.
Fair	50–69 percent of the students can perform the rhythm patterns with much assistance from the teacher.	The students can only tell the story of *Peter and the Wolf* accurately with much assistance from the teacher.
Novice	Fewer than 49 percent of the students can perform the rhythm patterns successfully, even with much assistance from the teacher.	The students cannot accurately tell the story of *Peter and the Wolf*, even with much assistance from the teacher.

Follow-up: Using flyers or e-mail announcements, advertise to parents that your students created an audio file or podcast representing their understanding of Prokofiev's *Peter and the Wolf*. The next time your students come to music class, play them their podcast on the website.

Items to Be Purchased: If you own a computer with recording capabilities and Internet access, and you use the podOmatic website (http://www.podomatic.com) to publish your podcast, then you will not need to purchase any items for this lesson to be successful.

Download from www.ti-me.org/TIEMC:
- "Peter.jpg"
- "Bird.jpg"
- "Duck.jpg"
- "Cat.jpg"
- "Wolf.jpg"
- "Grandpa.jpg"
- "Hunters.jpg"
- "Podcast_Peter_And_The_Wolf.pdf"
- "Podcast_Rubric.doc"

MENC Standards:	4. Composing and arranging music within specified guidelines.
TI:ME Technology Areas:	2. Music production

Experimenting with Sound Waves

By Karen Garrett, the 2006 TI:ME Teacher of the Year
Central Park School, Birmingham, Alabama
If you enjoy Karen's lessons, please check out her website for more lessons and excellent resources:
http://www.musictechteacher.com

Grade Level: Grades 2–5

Teacher's Technical Ability: Intermediate

Objective:
1. Students will expand their own composition (A-B-A song form) using the notes in the C-major scale, and the keyboard and sequencing software on the computer to play back the song.
2. Students will complete a brief study on sound waves and applications.

Materials/Equipment:
- Keyboards and related equipment.
- Computers (with or without Internet access).
- Printer.
- Sibelius (http://www.sibelius.com) or Music Time Deluxe (http://www.gvox.com).
- Computer microphones.
- Microsoft's Windows Media Player (with PCs) or Apple's iTunes (with Macs) in order to listen to the audio files.
- Sony's Acid Music Studio (for PC only) or Audacity (for PC and Mac) to record and edit the sound files.
- CD-R disks.
- Audio examples for this lesson can be found on Karen's website (http://www.musictechteacher.com).
- "Ask students to notice" sheet can be found on the TI:ME website (see "Download from www.ti-me.org/TIEMC") for printing.

Duration: These are plans or supplemental lessons in addition to our studies in Harmonic Vision's Music Ace, Sibelius, and the Alfred Piano Method Books. Each lesson or project can cover from one to three weeks of music classes. Each student receives a 40-minute lesson per week. Currently, I have 200 students in the second through fifth grades.

Prior Knowledge and Skills: The students will have composed a melody using the notes C, D, E, F, and G.

Procedure:
1. Students should learn what a sound wave is and how it is used in computer applications. Wave: The shape of a sound produced by an oscillator that determines the timbre of the sound. Waveforms include sine, pulse, sawtooth, square, and triangle waves. Sound wave: The shape of a sound, which can be illustrated on a graph. When something vibrates, variations in air pressure create vibrations and are transmitted as a sound wave. Different sounds have differently shaped waves.
2. Notice the sound wave lesson graphics below.
3. Students will use a microphone to record their voices into Sony's Acid Music Studio program on a Windows computer. Adjust the volume as needed. Let the student experiment with the sound wave by pressing "Effects" and "Echo," "Reverse," "Increase and Decrease Speed" (if you are using Audacity, press "Effect" and "Echo," "Reverse," and "Change Tempo").
4. The student should save their work in "My Documents."
5. Explain to the students how the digital version of their voices—the sound waves—are produced and recorded to CDs.
6. Many times, you will have to change the "Properties" of the sound wave to CD-quality audio format in order for it to be recorded to a CD-R disk.
7. If time is available, record the voices to a CD and play it back in a regular audio CD player.
8. Tell the students about the differences in MIDI and sound wave files. MIDI files have to be converted to sound waves using a mixer and other instrument, such as a keyboard, to record the file as a sound wave into the computer before it can be recorded to a CD.

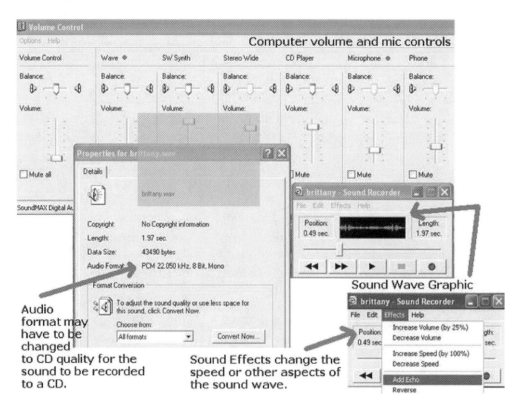

Fig. 2.16: Wave form properties and graphics.

9. Ask students to notice... (This can also be found on the TI:ME website as "Sound_Waves.pdf")
   a. What kinds of "shapes" are made when a voice is digitized on the computer?

b. Does your voice sound different than you think it does when you are speaking?
c. Does the sound wave that you made look like the sound waves that other students made? Why?
d. What are your favorite "effects" for changing your sound wave?
e. What happens when you speed up/slow down the sound wave?
f. Can a MIDI sound file be recorded to a CD like a digital sound wave?
g. Are sound waves larger in file size than MIDI files?
h. Can you find the starting point and ending point of your voice on the sound wave graphic?

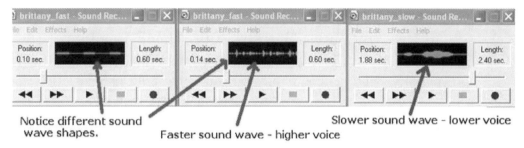

Fig. 2.17: The different shapes of sound waves.

11. Compositions: Students should expand their compositions in A-B-A song form. Remind students that A-B-A means you will write one section of the composition (part A), then write something different than your first section (part B), then write the first section of your song again (part A). In other words, part A repeats or is played twice. Write your composition using notes in the treble clef starting with middle C or higher, and use notes in the C-major scale. We will continue to have two staves or instrument voices playing. The students should not try to write the longest song in the world. Ask them to limit their compositions, for now, to 48–60 measures.

Evaluation:
1. Students will be able to name and play the notes to the C-major scale and use those notes to complete a composition in A-B-A form, using two staves, the General MIDI sound sheet, no longer than 48–60 measures.
2. Students will know how to use a microphone and the "Sound Recorder" in Windows to create a sound wave of their voice. Students will save their sounds to the computer and will demonstrate an understanding of what happens to the sound wave when they use "effects" to change the waveform.

Follow-up:
1. Follow this lesson with "Sound Waves and Cartoons Lesson."
2. Work on musical skills through some of the quizzes and games on the Music Tech Teacher Quizzes and Games pages at my website: (http://www.musictechteacher.com/musicquizzes.htm).
   a. Choose games according to the skill level of the students.
   b. There are several quizzes available for studying lines and spaces, rhythms, and skips, steps, repeats.
   c. There are a few Flash-based quizzes that use sound waves.

Items to Be Purchased: You will need software that can record and edit. If you have a PC, you can use Sony's Acid Music Studio (http://www.sonymediasoftware.com/products/acidfamily.asp). If you have a Mac, you can download the freeware Audacity (http://audacity.sourceforge.net/) to teach this lesson.

Download from www.ti-me.org/TIEMC: "Sound_Waves.pdf"

MENC Standards:	4. Composing and arranging music within.
TI:ME Technology Areas:	2. Music production
	5. Multimedia

Sound Waves and Cartoons Lesson

By Karen Garrett, 2006 TI:ME Teacher of the Year
Central Park School, Birmingham, Alabama

If you enjoy Karen's lessons, please check out her website for more lessons and excellent resources:
http://www.musictechteacher.com

Grade Level:	Grades 2–5
Teacher's Technical Ability:	Advanced
Objective:	1. To review the brief study on sound waves and applications.
	2. To take the sound wave lesson and add the sound waves of students' voices to cartoon characters in Flash.
Materials/Equipment:	• Computer(s) with a recent edition of the full Adobe Macromedia Flash program (http://www.adobe.com/products/flash/flashpro/) installed (such as Flash MX2004 or higher).
	• VocaliseWav program, a plug-in extension to Flash.
	• Pre-made graphics to use with the VocaliseWav program. A few graphic heads are included with the purchase of VocaliseWav.
	• Microphones to record voices into the computer.
	• The "Ask students to notice" sheet can be also found on the TI:ME website (see "Download from www.ti-me.org/TIEMC") for printing.
	• Poem or literary excerpt.
Duration:	These are plans or supplemental lessons in addition to our studies in Harmonic Vision's Music Ace, Sibelius, and the Alfred Piano Method Books. Each lesson or project can cover from one to three weeks of music classes. Each student receives a 40-minute lesson per week. Currently, I have 200 students in the second through fifth grades.
Prior Knowledge and Skills:	1. Students should review what a sound wave is and how it is used in computer applications.
	2. Students should have completed the "Experimenting with Sound Waves" lesson before beginning this lesson. Students will use a microphone to record their voices into the Sound Recorder program on a Windows computer.

Procedure:

1. Students read a poem or literary excerpt of their choice.
2. Students record this information into the computer using a microphone. Using the VocaliseWav plug-in, the students import their voice into the Flash program and apply it to one of the cartoon characters.
3. Immediately after importing their voices, students can play their cartoon clips on their computers (see student video clip at: (http://www.musictechteacher.com/music_tech_lesson006_sound_waves_cartoon.htm).
4, The sounds/phonemes from their voices will match the words spoken by the computer.
5. Students should speak very clearly into the microphone so the mouth of the cartoon character will match their words.
6. If the phoneme does not match the voice, it can be changed on individual frames. There are approximately 12–30 frames-per-second created. The editing has to be completed before importing the final character into your Flash animation. A screen shot of the program is shown below (see Fig. 2.18).

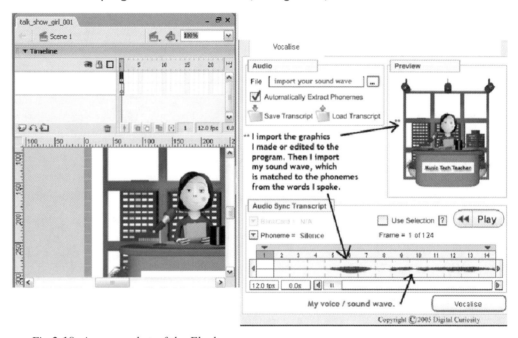

Fig 2.18: A screen shot of the Flash program.

7. Ask students to notice... (This can also be found on the TI:ME website as "Sound_Waves_Cartoons.pdf.")
   a. What kinds of "shapes" are made with the digitized voice on the computer?
   b. Does your voice sound different than you think it does when you are speaking?
   c. Does the sound wave that you made match the mouth movements of the cartoon? Why or why not?
   d. Can you find the starting and ending points of your voice on the sound wave graphic?
   e. Can you change the mouth movement on the cartoon if the phoneme does not match the voice? (Each frame can be changed to "repair" any words that did not form correctly.)

Evaluation:

1. Students will know how to use a microphone and the Sound Recorder in Windows to create a sound wave of their voice. Students will save their sounds to the computer and will demonstrate an understanding of what happens to the sound wave when they use effects to change the waveform.

2. Students will record their voices into their computers and import the sound into the Flash/VocaliseWav program. They will be able to add their voice to the cartoon character and save the file. (The students are not expected to create the cartoons, but to simply concentrate on the sound waves and phonemes.)

Follow-up: Work on musical skills through some of the quizzes and games on the Music Tech Teacher Quizzes and Games pages at the following website: http://www.musictechteacher.com/musicquizzes.htm.

    a. Choose games according to the skill level of the students.
    b. There are several quizzes available for studying lines and spaces, rhythms, and skips, steps, repeats.
    c. There are a few Flash-based quizzes that use sound waves.

Items to Be Purchased: Adobe Macromedia Flash (http://www.adobe.com/products/flash/flashpro/) and VocaliseWav, a plug-in extension to Flash.

Download from www.ti-me.org/TIEMC: "Sound_Waves_Cartoons.pdf"

"Skinny" Sound Effects

By Maedean Kramer
Far Hills Country Day School, Far Hills, New Jersey

Grade Level: Grades 4–6

Teacher's Technical Ability: Novice (if you use this lesson with keyboards)
Intermediate (if you use this lesson in a lab)

Objective: To explore the different nontraditional sounds/sound effects of a Korg keyboard and execute smooth transitions between sounds.

Materials/Equipment:
- Korg X50 keyboards.
- Korg Group Education Controller (GEC3—see Fig. 2.19) available through SoundTree (http://www.soundtree.com).
- Shel Silverstein's poem "Skinny," from *Where the Sidewalk Ends* (HarperCollins Children's Books, 1974).
- Rubric to evaluate students' orchestrations and executions (see "Download from www.ti-me.org/TIEMC").

Fig. 2.19: Korg Group Education Controller (GEC3).

Duration: 30–40 minutes

Prior Knowledge and Skills: This lesson is part of my "Lyrics and Pop Music" unit. Students listen to two modern songs that use sound effects to enhance their performances. Students should know how to change sounds within the various banks of the Korg X50 keyboards.

Procedure:
1. Hand out a copy of Shel Silverstein's poem "Skinny."
2. Have students read the poem aloud.
3. Students must find and underline five words or phrases for which they will create a sound accompaniment using sounds from the keyboard. (This will directly address substandard 4c from the MENC national standards: using a variety of sound sources when composing.)
4. Students choose five different sounds to enhance their words or phrases.
5. Have the students practice reading and orchestrating their versions of the poems.
6. Near the end of class, ask students to perform their poems for the class.

Evaluation: This rubric, which can be found on the TI:ME website, is based on a scale of 1–4, with 1 being the lowest point the students can achieve, and 4 being the highest.

Date_____

NAME_____

Orchestration:	Execution:
4: Students used five different sounds.	4: Students transitioned smoothly through all of the sounds.
3: Students used four different sounds.	3: Students transitioned smoothly through most of the sounds.
2: Students used three different sounds.	2: Students transitioned smoothly through some of the sounds.
1: Students used fewer than three different sounds.	1: Students transitioned smoothly through none of the sounds.

Follow-up: In this lesson, each student used the same poem. The next step is for students to choose another Shel Silverstein poem from *Where the Sidewalk Ends* to orchestrate. For the more advanced level, have students open up Apple's GarageBand, record their poem, and burn it to a CD for the educational purposes of self-evaluation and assessment.

Items to Be Purchased:
- Ideally, this lesson is performed in a keyboard lab with a GEC3 and one student per keyboard. This type of setup can be found at SoundTree (http://www.soundtree.com).
- *Finding Funds for Music Technology*, by Tom Rudolph (SoundTree, 1999), is an excellent resource for funding ideas.
- If you do not have a keyboard lab, this lesson can be adapted to fit any general music classroom with limited keyboard access.

Download from www.ti-me.org/TIEMC: "Skinny_Rubric.pdf"

MENC Standards:	2. Performing on instruments, alone and with others, a varied repertoire of music.
	3. Improvising melodies, variations, and accompaniments.
	4. Composing and arranging music within specified guidelines.
	6. Listening to, analyzing, and describing music.
	7. Evaluating music and musical performances.
	8. Understanding relationships between music, the other arts, and disciplines outside the arts.
TI:ME Technology Areas:	1. Electronic instruments
	5. Multimedia

A Symphony of Sounds: Creating Program Music

By Christine Dunleavy
Winslow Township Elementary School #5, Winslow Township, New Jersey

Grade Level:	Grades 4–6
Teacher's Technical Ability:	Intermediate
Objective:	Students will create "program music" based on sentences that can be musically represented. Using keyboards to select appropriate timbres/sound effects, they will create short melodies whose melodic contour, rhythm, tempo, and dynamics are meant to describe their sentences.
Materials/Equipment:	• A computer with an overhead projector.
	• Microsoft PowerPoint (http://office.microsoft.com/en-us/powerpoint/default.aspx) or Apple's Keynote (http://www.apple.com/iwork/keynote/) presentation that includes nouns and sentence examples. Printed pages and/or a regular overhead projector could be used. (See PowerPoint file in "Download from www.ti-me.org/TIEMC").
	• Electronic keyboards.
	• You will also need to make a grid handout for creating sentences and noting sounds (see pdf in "Download from www.ti-me.org/TIEMC").
Duration:	30 minutes
Prior Knowledge and Skills:	1. Students have already listened to examples of program music, such as Prokofiev's *Peter and the Wolf* or Saint-Saëns's *Carnival of the Animals*.
	2. Students have a basic understanding of musical elements.
	3. Students have some basic experience using keyboards.
Procedure:	1. Discuss program music and review familiar examples (*Peter and the Wolf*).
	2. Discuss inspiration for creating music, how elements can be used, etc.

3. Using the overhead, look at the list of nouns and go over sentence examples (you can use the pdf or PowerPoint files found on the TI:ME website):
   a. Determine appropriate sounds and find sound groups (use keyboards to check).
   b. Decide type of melodic contour, rhythm, tempo, and dynamics to fit the example.
4. Students can work alone or in pairs to write their own sentences on the grid handout, using the nouns from the list that you created (the grid handout can be found in the pdf file on the TI:ME website).
5. Students explore the keyboard to select sounds to use, writing the patch numbers on their grid sheets.
6. They improvise and create two- to four-bar melodies based on their sentences and play them for the class.
7. If time allows, students can create accompaniments (chords, percussion) for melodies.

Evaluation: Students demonstrate appropriate use of the following to musically represent the words and meaning of a sentence:
- Keyboard sounds (timbre/sound effects)
- Melodic contour
- Rhythm
- Tempo
- Dynamics

Rubric
Also found in the pdf file on the TI:ME website:
5: Creative use of all elements in a four-bar example
4: Same as above but shorter example
3: At least three elements are demonstrated properly
2: One element is used appropriately
1: No elements used

Follow-up:
1. Have the students play a guessing game (which sentence?) using each others' examples.
2. Have the class make up a chain story and link together program music examples.
3. Combine the examples and relate them to a musical form (A-B, A-B-A, rondo, etc.).
4. Notate or do alternative notation of the examples.
5. Record musical examples into a sequence program.
6. Create a multimedia presentation of examples:
   a. Enter into Notepad or Word
   b. Draw or Paint programs
   c. Import graphics, sound, etc.

Items to Be Purchased:
1. Keyboards
2. Computers with Microsoft's PowerPoint
3. Overhead projector

Download from www.ti-me.org/TIEMC:
- "A_Symphony_of_Sounds_Supplement.pdf" (includes all of the supplemental materials from the worksheets to the rubric)
- "A_Symphony_of_Sounds.ppt"

MENC Standards:	2. Performing on instruments, alone and with others, a varied repertoire of music.
	4. Composing and arranging music within specified guidelines.
	6. Listening to, analyzing, and describing music.
	8. Understanding relationships between music, the other arts, and disciplines outside the arts.
	9. Understanding music in relation to history and culture.
TI:ME Technology Areas:	1. Electronic instruments
	2. Music production
	6. Productivity tools/information processing/lab management

The Four Sacred Elements

By Amy Vanderwall
PS 334, New York City, New York

Grade Level: Grades 4–6

Teacher's Technical Ability: Novice

Objective: Fourth grade students will be able to identify the "Four Sacred Elements" (air, water, fire, earth), as found in Native American culture, and will be able to create a sound-scape representing one of the sacred elements based on their prior knowledge of Native American music and the universal elements of music (pitch, dynamics, duration, tempo, melody, and texture).

Materials/Equipment:
- Visual art representing the Four Sacred Elements:. See (http://www.tacoma .washington.edu/news/enews/feb04/The_Four_Elements.jpg) for an illustration depicting the four elements.
- Overhead or LCD projector to project the illustration of the four sacred elements onto a screen.
- Music representing the four sacred elements. Suggested: Mary Youngblood and Tito La Rosa, *The Prophecy of the Eagle and the Condor,* 2001. Songs: "Earth Spirit," "Fire Spirit," "Water Spirit," and "Wind Spirit."
- Apple iTunes free software (to play the music)—for PC and Mac (http://www.apple.com). CD player connected to the Korg GEC would also work well.
- Teacher Korg Group Education Controller 3 (GEC3—to manage class) (http://www.soundtree.com).
- Student headsets (to listen, respond, work with other students).
- Computers (two students/computer).
- Morton Subotnick's Creating Music software for soundscape project (http://www.creatingmusic.com).

Duration: 45 minutes

Prior Knowledge and Skills: This is the third lesson in a fourth grade Native American music unit. Students have already analyzed numerous Native American music examples and styles and have learned about Native American history and culture in social studies class and through their music lectures and discussions. In addition, the students are familiar with Morton Subotnick's Creating Music software. The overall Native American unit will fulfill the MENC content standards listed above.

Anticipatory Set:

1. Before the students enter the room, have the Four Sacred Elements image in PowerPoint or projected onto a screen via an overhead projector (no words, just image) and the four sacred elements music coming through the headsets. Note: Connect the teacher's computer to the LCD projector and GEC3. Have the image from the website projected onto the screen. Set the GEC3 to "LECTURE" and play the music in Apple iTunes.
2. Meet the students in the hall.
3. Tell them that there is music playing in their headsets, and an image projected on the screen.
4. As they walk in they should answer the following questions, "What do you see? What do you hear?"

Procedure:

1. After students have listened and are settled, turn the music down.
2. Ask, "What do you see? 'Call in' with your reflections." (The "Call" button on the GEC3 lets the students attract the teacher's attention without having to raise their hands. If you are performing this lesson in a different classroom setting, then having the students raise their hands and wait to be called on, will be fine.)
3. After students have responded, summarize what they have observed.
4. Ask, "What does this image represent? Call in with your ideas."
5. After students guess and/or respond with the representative elements, discuss how the Four Sacred Elements are an important aspect of Native American culture. (Answer: The sacred elements provide all that humans needed to survive.)
6. Ask students, "What do you hear? Call in with your reflections."
7. After students have responded, summarize what they have observed.
8. Show students the iTunes (or CD) music selection, which shows that each of the songs was created to represent one of the Four Sacred Elements (use the LCD projector if using iTunes). Discuss how the sacred elements were revered for their gifts and celebrated through music, art, dance, costume, storytelling, poetry, and other art forms (i.e., art forms were used to give thanks to the sacred elements, which sometimes took on human forms—such as those in the image projected).
9. Ask students to take out a piece of paper.
10. Ask students to write down the Four Sacred Elements.
11. Ask students to select one of the sacred elements and write five descriptive words for that element.
12. Ask students to write five different sounds that relate to their chosen element. Remind them to think about the instruments that were a part of Native American music and materials that were available to Native Americans to create sound and music. (Note: Native American instruments and natural materials were discussed in earlier classes.)
13. Tell students that they will now be using the Creating Music software to create a soundscape for their chosen element using their descriptive words and sounds. (Note: students should already be familiar with this software and creating sound-scapes in order to keep this lesson to 45 minutes.)
14. Tell students they will have the remainder of the class to work on this soundscape. The next class will be used for each soundscape presentation.
15. Students will need to turn in their descriptive sheet at the end of class, which will be returned the next class.

Evaluation: **Check for student understanding**
1. Collect the students' written words.
2. Check that all four elements were correctly identified.
3. Review the five descriptive words and five sounds for relevance. Make comments as necessary.

Closure

At the end of class, ask students, "What did we learn today?" Points that should be discussed include:

Naming the Four Sacred Elements.

Naming the art forms (music, visual art, etc.) that enabled Native Americans to recognize and honor the Four Sacred Elements.

Naming the numerous Native American instruments and materials that can be used to compose a soundscape representing one of the sacred elements.

Follow-up:
1. Have students draw/paint/sketch an image to go with their soundscape. This can be done in music class, or as a joint art class project.
2. Have students perform their soundscape using keyboard/MIDI music and/or real instruments.
3. Have students compose, notate, and perform a musical score (using Western musical notation) representing one (or all) of the Four Sacred Elements. Students should use their soundscape as a guide.
4. Have students write a poem and/or story about one of the Four Sacred Elements using their descriptive words, then compose a musical score or soundscape to perform with their written words. Students should first receive a mini-lesson on Native American poetry and/or storytelling. This could be done in music class, or as a joint English/social studies class project.

Items to Be Purchased: This lesson can be done without the Korg GEC3. If your school has a computer lab, you could purchase Morton Subotnick's Creating Music, which is an inexpensive software. For more information about this software, please see Morton Subotnick's website: http://www.creatingmusic.com.

Download from www.ti-me.org/TIEMC: None

MENC Standards:	4. Composing and arranging music within specified guidelines.
	6. Listening to, analyzing, and describing music.

TI:ME Technology Areas:	2. Music production

Finding and Manipulating MIDI Files in the General Music Class

By Dr. Thomas E. Rudolph
Haverford School District, Haverford, Pennsylvania

This article was previously published in the November 2005 issue of *Music Education Technology* magazine, a property of Penton Media, and is reprinted with the permission of its publisher.
http://metmagazine.com/mag/finding_manipulating_midi/

Grade Level:	Grades 5–6
Teacher's Technical Ability:	Advanced
Objective:	We will focus on two sets of skills: Downloading MIDI files from websites, and manipulating and arranging them using music-production/MIDI-sequencing software.
Materials/Equipment:	• Computer with Internet access • MIDI sequencer/music production software • MIDI files • Electronic keyboard (optional) Note: If you do not have access to the web in the classroom, then you can access the MIDI file "Fugue_in_Gminor.mid" from the TI:ME website and utilize the second and third parts of this lesson.
Duration:	Three class periods (30–45 minutes)
Procedure:	**Part 1: Finding MIDI Files** 1. The first part of this lesson involves teaching students to search for and download MIDI files from the Internet. a. For example, if you are teaching a unit on the classical era, you might require students to locate MIDI files composed by Mozart. 2. Students can search for MIDI files by doing a Google search (http://www.google.com) and entering the composer's name and the word "MIDI" in the search box. 3. Another option is to have the students visit specific sites that offer MIDI files. For classical music, I recommend the Choral Public Domain website (http://www.cpdl.org) and the Classical MIDI Archives (http://www.classicalarchives.com); but there are many other good choices. 4. The Classical MIDI Archives requires users to register in order to download files. A free subscription is available to anyone who has an email address, but it has a download limit of five files per day. Unlimited files can be downloaded for a $25 annual fee.

5. On most websites containing MIDI files, if you click the mouse button (or left-click with a two-button mouse) on a hyperlink, the file will stream—that is, it will play back, in real time, through your computer's built-in synthesizer (usually a software synth or a sound card's synth chip).

6. To download the file to the computer's hard drive, right-click (Windows) or Control-click (Mac) on the link to the selected MIDI file.

7. Be sure to instruct students to name and save the file to a familiar location on their hard drives, such as the "My Documents" folder.

   a. If there is no Internet connection available to the students in your classroom, you can download selected MIDI files ahead of time, then copy them to the student computers.

Part 2: Arranging with MIDI Files

1. After the desired file is downloaded, the students should open it using a MIDI sequencer or other program that can import and edit MIDI files.

   a. Examples of such programs include MOTU Digital Performer, Steinberg Cubase, Propellerhead Reason, Apple GarageBand, Cakewalk Sonar Home Studio, and Ableton Live. Consult the software's documentation for the specific steps to import a MIDI file.

2. Once the file is imported into the software, students can manipulate and arrange the file according to specific guidelines.

   a. For example, you can have then experiment by changing the synthesizer sounds used to play the tracks. Give students some direction, such as, "Select instruments that would have been used by the composer."

   b. Another option is to create a modern version of the piece with newer instrumentation.

3. Although it sounds dated today, you could play selections from Wendy Carlos's famous *Switched on Bach* (CBS Records, 1968) to give students ideas about how they might adjust the music through tempo and timbre.

Part 3: Adding Tracks

1. If your sequencing program can manipulate audio and MIDI loops (a feature almost all modern sequencers have), instruct the students to add some percussion loops to the file to change the style or feel of the piece. Start with drum and percussion loops, because they do not require transposition.

2. Horn, wind, and string loops will need to be carefully added to the sequence, because the students will have to match the loop's key with that of the sequence.

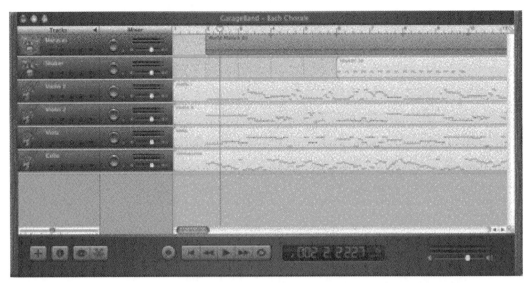

Fig. 2.20: This MIDI file, shown in Apple's GarageBand 2, has been enhanced by adding MIDI loops.

3. I like to have students first record a live percussion track. Adding harmonic parts can be more difficult for some students as it requires an understanding of harmony.

The Benefits: This lesson will unlock some very important areas for students. They will learn how to use the Internet to locate MIDI files, and manipulating MIDI files will help them to become aware of the instrumentation, form, and many other aspects of the piece. Finally, arranging and adding new tracks helps students move toward the eventual goal of recording their own original sequences.

Download from www.ti-me.org/TIEMC: "Fugue_in_Gminor.mid"

MENC Standards:	2.	Performing on instruments, alone and with others, a varied repertoire of music.
	4.	Composing and arranging music within specified guidelines.
	5.	Reading and notating music.
	6.	Listening to, analyzing, and describing music.
	7.	Evaluating music and musical performances.
	8.	Understanding relationships between music, the other arts, and disciplines outside the arts.
	9.	Understanding music in relation to history and culture.
TI:ME Technology Areas:	1.	Electronic instruments
	3.	Notation software
	5.	Multimedia
	7.	Web/Internet

The Blues: A Creative Experience in American Music

By Amy Vanderwall
PS 334, New York City, New York

Grade Level: Grades 5–6

Teacher's Technical Ability: Intermediate

Objective: The overall goal of this activity is to present students with a problem that they have to solve by creating their own version of a traditional musical form: the blues. Students will first learn the history of the blues and the basic structure and scale used in most blues tunes. Then, in small groups, students will create their own blues composition. Students will evaluate each other for a final project grade.

Materials/Equipment:
- Overview of Jazz at Lincoln Center (http://www.jazzatlincolncenter.org/).
- Reference materials that introduce the history and works of the blues. Suggested materials:
  Books
  The Sound that Jazz Makes by C.B. Weatherford, C.B (Walker & Co., 2000).
  Blues Singers: Ten Who Rocked the World by J. Lester (Jump at the Sun/Hyperion Books for Children., 2001).
  Websites
  Jazz at Lincoln Center Curriculum, Lesson 4: "The Blues"
  (http://www.jalc.org/jazzED/j4yp_curr/modules/theBlues/module.html).
  The Blues Foundation, "What Is the Blues?"
  (http://www.blues.org/blues/index.php4).
- A computer with Internet access, hooked up to a TV or LCD projector with a screen.
- Notation software (optional).
- The evaluation, which can be found as a pdf file on the TI:ME website (see "Download from www.ti-me.org/TIEMC").

Recordings:

Era	Song	Artist	Album	Album Year
'20s/'30s	"Mountain Jack Blues"	Ma Rainey	Madam Gertrude "Ma" Rainey: 1923–1928	1997
'20s/'30s	"St. Louis Blues"	Bessie Smith	Bessie Smith: The Collection	1989
'40s/'50s	"Stormy Blues"	Billie Holiday	The Complete Billie Holiday Verve: 1945–1959	1993
'50s	"Rockin' Chair"	Fats Domino	The Early Imperial Singles 1950–52	1996
'50s/'60s	"Mannish Boy"	Muddy Waters	Muddy "Mississippi" Waters Live	1989
'60s	"Red House"	Jimi Hendrix	Music from the Motion Picture "City of Angels"	1998
'70s	"Bad to the Bone"	George Thorogood & The Destroyers	The Baddest of George Thorogood & The Destroyers	1992
'90s	"Mr. Cab Driver"	Lenny Kravitz	Lenny Kravitz Greatest Hits	2000

- Electronic keyboards or any melodic instrument (such as an xylophone or a wood-wind, brass, or string instrument).
- Music staff paper.
- Whiteboard/markers or chalkboard/chalk.
- Paper for student journals.

Duration: Teachers should assess their own class needs, but projected timing is as follows:
1. Lesson: two 45-minute periods
2. Challenge (introduction, student group work, and performance/evaluation): four 45-minute classes

Prior Knowledge and Skills: Students should have basic performance skills in a melodic instrument, and should possess a basic understanding of music notation.

Procedure:
1. Ask students, "What are the blues?" Jot down the students' ideas on the board. There are no right or wrong answers. This will provide a starting point for the lesson.
2. Introduce the history of the blues using the resource materials above. Students should recognize:
   - The blues originated in the African-American slave work songs and spirituals. With the end of slavery, the blues traveled across the United States with the "traveling blues men and women" who moved from rural to urban centers. The blues sound also developed further in African-American churches via gospel music. There is no exact map of its early history as it was passed orally. The first recordings of the blues were made in the 1920s. Jazz was born out of the blues.
   - The blues is a feeling that is expressed through the music—usually about a sadness or a difficult life experience, but it can be about anything.
   - The blues is also a standard form and sound of "blue notes."

3. Introduce the standard 12-bar blues form and the blues scale. Examples in the key of C are noted below. Emphasize that the standard form has evolved over time and that many blues musicians stray from the form, but it is still used today. Highlight the "blue notes" of the blues scale and that these notes are the telltale signs that a tune is a blues tune. Have the students play the standard form (use root of each chord) and the scale to gain a general feel for the blues on the electronic keyboards.

The standard 12-bar blues—in C:
Measures 1–4: C, C, C, C
Measures 5–8: F, F, C, C
Measures 9–12: G, F, C, C

The C blues scale:
C–E♭ (blue note)–F–G♭ (blue note)–G– B♭–C

4. Listen to the blues (at least two choruses of at least three different selections). All of the recommended listening excerpts are in the standard 12-bar blues form with the exception of "Bad to the Bone" and "Mannish Boy," which can be introduced as a nonstandard blues. These tunes will probably be familiar to most students. Ask the students what they hear. Collect ideas on the board. Again, there are no wrong answers.

5. Select one standard tune to listen to more intently. Have the students follow the blues standard form in the song. In addition, ask the students what they notice about the lyrics. After this exercise, students should recognize that:
   - Lyrics are in an A-A-B form. The first line is sung for four bars, then repeated (call and response).
   - Vocalists let their personality shine using slang ("yonda") or asides ("lord") to emphasize the emotion.
   - The blues lyrics usually tell a story.
   - Instrumental solos for twelve bars are often found in between twelve bars of lyrics.

Problem/Challenge/ Evaluation/Conclusion:

1. Introduce the students to the Jazz at Lincoln Center (JLC) Orchestra directed by Wynton Marsalis. Students should recognize that:
   - JLC was created to educate the public, especially young people, about the rich heritage of jazz, its great works and musicians, and the relationship between jazz and other disciplines.
   - The JLC Orchestra holds concerts that present a myriad of jazz themes from the blues and Latin jazz to the work of jazz composers like Duke Ellington and Paul Whitman.

2. Present the "problem": The JLC Orchestra directed by Wynton Marsalis needs a composition to present at their (pretend) upcoming concert, "The Blues: An American Musical Tradition."

3. Present the "challenge": Based on their study of the blues, in groups of two or three, students must compose a blues tune for the upcoming concert. The minimum perameters:
   - There must be a title.
   - There must be a clear 12-bar blues melody that can be played on their melodic instrument. The melody must be created from the blues scale and written out on staff paper.

- There must be at least two choruses of lyrics also written out on staff paper (this can also be done with notation software).
- The group must perform their blues tune for the class (teacher should tell students their time frame).

Evaluation: 1. Have students design their own evaluation tool.
- Have students brainstorm about what makes a "good" blues tune. List ideas on the board.
- Summarize and/or vote as necessary so you have five categories. Assign each category a value.
- Create an evaluation worksheet. Students will grade each other on the day of the performances.
- Example evaluation (this evaluation can also be printed from the TI:ME website—see "Download from www.ti-me.org/TIEMC"):

GROUP
MEMBERS:_____

Component	Possible Points	Points Given	Comments
Clear 12-bar form and original use of the blues scale	10		
Original lyrics/story	10		
Instrumental presentation (technique, emotion, addition of solos, originality, etc.)	10		
Vocal presentation (technique, emotion, etc.)	10		
Musical score (rhythm, notation, lyrics, etc.)	10		
Total	**50**		
Would you send this tune to the Jazz at Lincoln Center Orchestra?	yes	no	(circle on and comment)

2. Have students divide into groups. Provide students with music staff paper. Students should begin working in their small groups with the teacher providing guidance as necessary.
3. Have students perform their blues composition for the rest of the class. Ensure that copies of the compositions are given to each student. After each performance, the class should evaluate each performance based on the class evaluation. Final scores will be tallied outside of class by the teacher (or helpers with teacher oversight) and presented to each student in the next class.
4. To conclude this activity, have students write in their journals what they learned about the blues and what they experienced during their problem solving time.

Follow-up: 1. Have students draw/paint/sketch an image to go with their composition. This can be done in music class, or as a joint art class project.
2. Have students write a few verses of lyrics to their composition using the A-A-B blues lyrical form, slang, and asides. Students should try to tell a story with their lyrics, and let their personality shine while singing! Have students perform their lyrics for the class.

3. Have students improvise using the C blues scale on their melodic instrument, and incorporate solos into their blues composition.
4. Record student work for analysis and review. You could use audio software such as the freeware Audacity. (http://audacity.sourceforge.net/), for Mac or PC; or Apple's GarageBand (http://www.apple.com/ilife/garageband/), for Mac only.
5. This is a great unit to use within a larger study of jazz music. From this unit, you can proceed into other styles of jazz and/or connect to many other popular styles of music (rap, R&B, gospel, etc.).

Items to Be Purchased: The teacher must have a computer with Internet access, and either a CD player or iTunes (freeware for PC and Mac at http://www.apple.com) to play the musical recordings.

Download from www.ti-me.org/TIEMC: "Blues_Evaluation.pdf"

MENC Standards:	2. Performing on instruments, alone and with others, a varied repertoire of music.
	3. Improvising melodies, variations, and accompaniments.
	4. Composing and arranging music within specified guidelines.
	7. Evaluating music and musical performances.
	9. Understanding music in relation to history and culture.
TI:ME Technology Areas:	1. Electronic instruments
	2. Music production

Composing with the Blues

By Stefani Langol
Assistant Professor of Music Education, Berklee College of Music,
Berklee, Massachusetts

This article was previously published in the April 2005 issue of *Music Education Technology* magazine,
a property of Penton Media, and is reprinted with the permission of its publisher.
http://metmagazine.com/lessonplan/composing_blues/

Grade Level: Grades 5–6

Teacher's Technical Ability: Advanced

Objective: In this lesson, our goals are to give students a historical framework of the blues, provide a basic knowledge of the 12-bar blues form and harmonic progression, and offer the opportunity for students to create their own 12-bar blues songs using any digital audio sequencer (such as Cakewalk Sonar Home Studio, Steinberg's Cubase (http://www .steinberg.net), or Apple's GarageBand (http://www.apple.com/ilife/garageband/). By the end of the lesson, students will record drums, a bass line, an accompaniment part, and a vocal track with original lyrics.

Materials/Equipment: There are a variety of materials/equipment that can be used for this lesson. To see a complete list, please see "Items to Be Purchased."

Duration: 3–4 class periods

Prior Knowledge and Skills: The lesson assumes that students have a basic working knowledge of the software you are using, a basic knowledge of the pentatonic or blues scale, and a familiarity with I, IV, and V chords, basic rhythms, and rhythmic subdivision in 4/4 time. You can also accomplish this project by providing MIDI and audio loops (recorded musical phrases that repeat seamlessly).

Procedure: **First Steps**
1. Begin by establishing the historical and musical context for the project. There are some excellent teaching strategies and learning resources available on the Internet that you can use to assist with the integration of blues music, its culture, and its history into the classroom (see "Blues on the Web" in the "Items to Be Purchased" list).

2. Create a blues WebQuest for your students to use (see "Glossary" at the end of this book). WebQuests provide students with an online research experience that will greatly enrich their learning.
3. Discuss and analyze the basic 12-bar blues form and harmonic progression. A simple 12-bar blues progression typically uses the I, IV, and V chords and consists of three 4-bar phrases. For a graphic showing two common three-chord progressions, go to the TI:ME website.
   a. Examine several blues lyrics and discuss writing original lyrics for a 12-bar blues. Blues lyrics often tell a story and follow an A-A-B pattern.

Creating the tracks
1. Students can create their own 12-bar blues song using a program like GarageBand or Home Studio. Your project should contain at least four tracks: bass, harmonic accompaniment, drums, and lead vocal.
2. You may want the students to add a fifth track for an improvised lead. Students can create these tracks in a variety of ways, and the process will be determined by the teacher's curricular goals.
3. Tracks can be MIDI recordings, audio recordings, or prerecorded MIDI or audio loops (see Fig. 2.21). For instance, they could use an electronic keyboard to record the bass, drums, and harmonic accompaniment MIDI tracks, recording the vocals on an audio track.

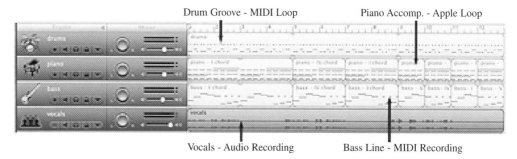

Fig. 2.21: This piece, recorded in Apple's GarageBand digital audio sequencer, includes MIDI tracks, linear audio tracks, and audio loops.

   a. In case you don't have a program like GarageBand or Home Studio that comes with library of loops, there are lots of free MIDI and audio loops available on the Web, as well as numerous, inexpensive loop packages you can purchase.

4. Once the project has been recorded and arranged, students can use the digital audio sequencer's MIDI- and audio-editing tools to make changes or correct mistakes.

Finishing up
1. The next step is to mix the song.
2. Mixing is the art of creating a balance between all of the tracks in a project. Setting volumes, panning tracks to the left or right, adjusting tone with EQ, and adding effects such as reverb are all part of the mixing process.

Evaluation: Once the project is completed, students should share and evaluate their tunes. If possible, archive their creations by burning a CD or posting the files to the school website.

Items to Be Purchased: You can find many materials for this lesson online, for free.

1. Blues on the Web

The Web is a great source of information on the blues. The sites listed here are just a few examples to get you started:

- **Blue Highway**: www.thebluehighway.com
- **How the Blues Affected Race Relations in the United States**: www.jessicagrant.net/thesis/index.html
- **PBS History of the Blues** (includes lesson-plan material): www.pbs.org/theblues/classroom.html
- **The History of Blues Music**: http://afroamhistory.about.com/library/weekly/aa030501a.htm

2. Free loops

You can buy some excellent commercial loop libraries, and a number of programs let you create your own loops. But if you look around on the Web, you can also find free, downloadable loops, which can be a real time-saver. Here are a few sites to check out:

- **Free Loops**: www.freeloops.com
- **Groove Monkee**: www.groovemonkee.com/
- **Looperman Audio Resources**: www.looperman.com/loops_samples_menu.php
- **Partners in Rhyme**: www.partnersinrhyme.com

Download from www.ti-me.org/TIEMC: None

MENC Standards:	2. Performing on instruments, alone and with others, a varied repertoire of music.
	4. Composing and arranging music within specified guidelines.
	5. Reading and notating music.
	6. Listening to, analyzing, and describing music.
	7. Evaluating music and musical performances.

TI:ME Technology Areas:	2. Music production
	3. Notation software
	5. Multimedia
	6. Productivity tools/information processing/lab management
	7. Web/Internet

It's Elementary: A Video Project—Part 1

ACTIVITY 1: STAFF PAPER AND INSTRUMENT

This project has six activities. To utilize this lesson to its fullest, please read all six.

By Maureen Spranza

San Lorenzo Unified School District at Hillside Elementary School, Hayward, California

This article was previously published in the June 2004 issue of *Music Education Technology* magazine, a property of Penton Media, and is reprinted with the permission of its publisher.
http://metmagazine.com/mag/elementary/

Grade Level:	Grades K–6

Teacher's Technical Ability:	Advanced

Before We Begin:	Before we get started with this project, let us recognize that many teachers do not yet have the resources to publish pages to the Internet. Furthermore, video is more difficult to produce and post than audio, and the quality of streaming video (and sometimes audio) over the Internet depends on the speed of one's Internet connection. In addition, as we will discuss shortly, permission release forms are always needed before posting student work or images, and you might also need to consider privacy and security issues (see "It's Elementary: A Video Project—Part 6"). If any of these considerations are problematic for you, do not give up on the project. Instead, use your creativity to design a variation that works for you and your program.
	Teachers who lack access to a school website are not necessarily left out in the cold. Web-hosting services such as http://myhosting.com are available for as little as $9.95 a month, allowing you to have your own website relatively inexpensively. Currently, Wikispaces, at http://www.wikispaces.com, allows you to create simple Web pages that groups, friends, and families can edit together for free (public wikis) or a small fee (private and ad-free wikis).

Finally, teachers should always monitor any student who is using the Internet. Good Web-monitoring practices will quickly become second nature, as with other important everyday safety precautions.

Overall Objective: The overall objective of this six-part lesson is to create streaming performance videos and original music compositions for publication on the school's website.

Materials/Equipment: This project is most easily accomplished if you have your own classroom. If you are an itinerant teacher, some aspects might be a bit inconvenient, but the project can still be practical and worthwhile. Here is what you will need.

- Pencils, erasers, and composition-paper templates for everyone in the class. Using a different template for each grade level helps achieve the necessary benchmarks. For instance, in second grade the template can be big enough to allow the children to write their own words. In third grade, I like students to compose a song flute duet, and in fifth grade, we use a template for a 12-bar keyboard blues. In my classroom, the children store their work in a folder, including reference materials with the names of the music symbols we have covered and the symbols' relationships to their instruments.
- A sufficient supply of glockenspiels with mallets, song flutes, recorders, or small keyboards. It might also be helpful to have some music stands. Students can work in pairs or teams, if necessary, to stretch your limited supply of instruments.
- Four desktop computers, complete with USB ports, sound card, speakers, head-phones, and at least one computer with a composite-video adapter for connecting your computer to a TV.
- The computers should have Internet access and Finale NotePad freeware (http://www.finalemusic.com). It is also great to have a network server, because that allows students to save their work to a place where you can directly access it from your computer. As we will see, though, there are some caveats regarding younger children having access to a file server.
- You will need Web-publishing software, such as Adobe Macromedia Dreamweaver (http://www.adobe.com/products/dreamweaver/) or iWeb (http://www.apple.com/ilife) (for Mac only).
- You might also want a scanner and CD-R blanks for saving student work.
- In order to make a 30-second video, you will need a low-cost video camera or webcam.
- You will also need an inexpensive dynamic microphone with either a 1/8-inch jack or a 1/4-inch jack and 1/8-inch adapter, which you will plug into the sound card. Budget mics are available for as little as $10, although at that price, the quality will be relatively poor. If you can afford $80 to $100 for a better mic, such as a Shure SM-58 (http://www.shure.com), you will get much better recordings.

Duration: Six to eight class periods to complete all six activities.

Prior Knowledge and Skills: Basic rhythm and composition skills such as note values, form, and meter. In addition, the students need the ability to play a glockenspiel and to use a computer.

Procedure: **Activity 1: Staff Paper and Instrument**
1. The first step in activity 1 is for the teacher and students to compose a model together on the white board or on an overhead of the template. For the lower grades, I like to divide the composition into A-B-A form, using the analogy of an Oreo cookie. In the A section, the children are only allowed to use the "chocolate"

quarter notes, eighth notes, and quarter rests (or "ta," "ti-ti," and "ta" rests). In the the B section, children are asked to use the cream notes, such as the white (uncolored) whole note and half note.

    a. If you are working with kindergartners, you may only want to start with a three-measure A-B-A composition. In that way, the children would choose either one whole note or two half notes for their B section. As you move up the grade levels with lengthier compositions, the children would be able to use both whole notes and half notes in their compositions.

2. It is helpful to break down the composition process into a series of simple steps so that the children do not get overwhelmed. The questions to ask children are as follows:

    a. Do you want a rest or a note?

    b. Which rest or note do you want?

    c. If it is a note, which letter/pitch do you want: C, E, G, or A; F, A, C, or D; do, mi, sol, or la?

    d. What number does the symbol stand for? How many beats?

    e. Does it add up to the number of beats per measure that the time signature indicates?

3. After you model the process, you can use direct instruction to have the children compose a piece together. The students can then compose a second piece independently.

4. Encourage the students to sing the notes and chant "ta" and "ti-ti," as well as play their instruments. They will work hard to finish their composition as they look forward to their turn on the software to create their composition Web page!

5. Students get three points in red pen on their paper when they finish, and they are then assigned to one of the four computers in the room. If all four computers are in use with students starting activity 2 (see "It's Elementary: A Video Project—Part 2"), then he or she can skip to activity 3 (see "It's Elementary: A Video Project—Part 3") and be put on a waiting list for activity 2.

Evaluation: The students will compose their own compositions with guided rhythms and notes in A-B-A form.

Follow-up: "It's Elementary: A Video Project—Part 2"

Download from www.ti-me.org/TIEMC:
- "2nd_ABA_Glockenspiel_Template.pdf"
- "3rd_Grade_Song_Flute_Duet_ABA. pdf"
- "3rd_template_w_IIVV.pdf "
- "4th_Recorder_Composition. pdf"
- "4th_Grade_Recorder_Fingerings. pdf"
- "5th_template_piano. pdf"
- "Grades_345_comp_checklist.pdf"

MENC Standards:	2. Performing on instruments, alone and with others, a varied repertoire of music.
	4. Composing and arranging music within specified guidelines.
	5. Reading and notating music.
	6. Listening to, analyzing, and describing music.
	7. Evaluating music and musical performances.
TI:ME Technology Areas:	2. Music production
	3. Notation software
	5. Multimedia
	6. Productivity tools/information processing/lab management
	7. Web/Internet

It's Elementary: A Video Project—Part 2
ACTIVITY 2: FINALE NOTEPAD
By Maureen Spranza
San Lorenzo Unified School District at Hillside Elementary School, Hayward, California
This article was previously published in the June 2004 issue of *Music Education Technology* magazine,
a property of Penton Media, and is reprinted with the permission of its publisher.
http://metmagazine.com/mag/elementary/

Grade Level:	Grades K–6
Teacher's Technical Ability:	Advanced
Overall Objective:	The overall objective of this six-part lesson is to create streaming performance videos and original music compositions for publication on the school's website.
Materials/Equipment:	This project is most easily accomplished if you have your own classroom. If you are an itinerant teacher, some aspects might be a bit inconvenient, but the project can still be practical and worthwhile. Here is what you will need.

- Pencils, erasers, and composition-paper templates for everyone in the class. Using a different template for each grade level helps achieve the necessary benchmarks. For instance, in second grade the template can be big enough to allow the children to write their own words. In third grade, I like students to compose a song flute duet, and in fifth grade, we use a template for a 12-bar keyboard blues. In my classroom, the children store their work in a folder, including reference materials with the names of the music symbols we have covered and the symbols' relationships to their instruments.
- A sufficient supply of glockenspiels with mallets, song flutes, recorders, or small keyboards. It might also be helpful to have some music stands. Students can work in pairs or teams, if necessary, to stretch your limited supply of instruments.

- Four desktop computers, complete with USB ports, sound card, speakers, headphones, and at least one computer with a composite-video adapter for connecting your computer to a TV.
- The computers should have Internet access and Finale NotePad freeware (http://www.finalemusic.com). It is also great to have a network server, because that allows students to save their work to a place where you can directly access it from your computer. As we will see, though, there are some caveats regarding younger children having access to a file server.
- You will need Web-publishing software, such as Adobe Macromedia Dreamweaver (http://www.adobe.com/products/dreamweaver/) or iWeb (http://www.apple.com/ilife) (for Mac only).
- You might also want a scanner and CD-R blanks for saving student work.
- In order to make a 30-second video, you will need a low-cost video camera or webcam.
- You will also need an inexpensive dynamic microphone with either a 1/8-inch jack or a 1/4-inch jack and 1/8-inch adapter, which you will plug into the sound card. Budget mics are available for as little as $10, although at that price, the quality will be relatively poor. If you can afford $80 to $100 for a better mic, such as a Shure SM-58 (http://www.shure.com), you will get much better recordings.

Duration: Six to eight class periods to complete all six activities.

Prior Knowledge and Skills: Basic rhythm and composition skills such as note values, form, and meter. In addition, the students need the ability to play a glockenspiel and to use a computer.

Procedure:

Activity 2: Finale Notepad

1. The Finale NotePad freeware is perfect for use with elementary students. Since the MENC standards do not ask the children to get too detailed or extravagant, Finale NotePad's features are sufficient for the children to accomplish the benchmarks successfully.

2. For this activity, it is a good idea to have your computer hooked up to a TV display or a projector. The first step depends on the rules in your school district about downloading and installing software. If you are allowed to install software, you can start by showing the children how to download a copy of Finale NotePad. Keep a record of which classes have seen it downloaded and installed. This is helpful for students who have never downloaded a program or have never seen one downloaded.

3. After downloading NotePad, students should be shown how to click on "Remind Me Later" when it asks you to register, and "Continue" when it asks if you would like to purchase anything else. Next, show students how to input their title and name. Small children need to be reminded that capital letters must be used in titles, and that they are made with the shift key on the keyboard.
   a. If you are not allowed to install software on school computers, just forge ahead with the copies of NotePad that the school's computer tech has installed on your classroom computers. You also can send the children home with a letter to their parents introducing Finale NotePad and providing instructions for installing the program on the family computer, if they have one.

4. With the software installed, the next step is to show students how to fill in the rest of the wizard, including instrument family, instrument, key signature, and time signature. Many younger children need to have a template of the Finale NotePad file with the time signature, key signature, and so on already filled in. Older elementary students, such as fifth graders, are better able to handle those tasks.

5. Once NotePad is set up, it is time to model how to input notes and rests according to the rules of the project. Then you can show the students how to play the music and save their work to the server or hard drive as .mus and html files. Of course, students will need to know how to find their saved work when they return to the computer, so show them where the work is saved. I create a student work folder on my hard drive every year, and inside that folder are folders for every teacher's class by grade level, such as "3 Smith." If children are working with individual laptops, this activity can be taken one step further by using direct instruction in order to have the children go through the steps together.

6. It is important to recognize that children in grades three and lower have a difficult time saving files correctly, let alone saving them to a server and finding them again. Sometimes students accidentally click on the wrong files and even delete files with out realizing it, so you are well advised to supervise the students and their files when they are working on the computers. In addition, many children will have questions throughout the lesson, so be prepared to help with the computers while teaching the rest of your class.

7. Each time the children come to music class, you will need to make sure the kids are at the correct computer and are working on the right activity with the appropriate partner. If a student takes a long time completing their paper from the first activity, or is waiting a long time for their turn on the computer or the video, consider pairing him or her with faster students to help complete the project. If you feel it necessary, a slow student could use a scanner to input work, but that defeats one of our goals, which is to teach them to use a notation program.

Evaluation: The students will compose their own compositions with guided rhythms and notes in A-B-A form on the computer using Finale NotePad.

Follow-up: "It's Elementary: A Video Project—Part 3"

Download from www.ti-me.org/TIEMC: None

MENC Standards:	2. Performing on instruments, alone and with others, a varied repertoire of music.
	4. Composing and arranging music within specified guidelines.
	5. Reading and notating music.
	6. Listening to, analyzing, and describing music.
	7. Evaluating music and musical performances.
TI:ME Technology Areas:	2. Music production
	3. Notation software
	5. Multimedia
	6. Productivity tools/information processing/lab management
	7. Web/Internet

It's Elementary: A Video Project—Part 3
ACTIVITY 3: PRACTICING NOTES
By Maureen Spranza
San Lorenzo Unified School District at Hillside Elementary School, Hayward, California

This article was previously published in the June 2004 issue of *Music Education Technology* magazine,
a property of Penton Media, and is reprinted with the permission of its publisher.
http://metmagazine.com/mag/elementary/

Grade Level:	Grades K–6
Teacher's Technical Ability:	Advanced
Overall Objective:	The overall objective of this six-part lesson is to create streaming performance videos and original music compositions for publication on the school's website.
Materials/Equipment:	This project is most easily accomplished if you have your own classroom. If you are an itinerant teacher, some aspects might be a bit inconvenient, but the project can still be practical and worthwhile. Here is what you will need.

- Pencils, erasers, and composition-paper templates for everyone in the class. Using a different template for each grade level helps achieve the necessary benchmarks. For instance, in second grade the template can be big enough to allow the children to write their own words. In third grade, I like students to compose a song flute duet, and in fifth grade, we use a template for a 12-bar keyboard blues. In my classroom, the children store their work in a folder, including reference materials with the names of the music symbols we have covered and the symbols' relationships to their instruments.
- A sufficient supply of glockenspiels with mallets, song flutes, recorders, or small keyboards. It might also be helpful to have some music stands. Students can work in pairs or teams, if necessary, to stretch your limited supply of instruments.

- Four desktop computers, complete with USB ports, sound card, speakers, headphones, and at least one computer with a composite-video adapter for connecting your computer to a TV.
- The computers should have Internet access and Finale NotePad freeware (http://www.finalemusic.com). It is also great to have a network server, because that allows students to save their work to a place where you can directly access it from your computer. As we will see, though, there are some caveats regarding younger children having access to a file server.
- You will need Web-publishing software, such as Adobe Macromedia Dreamweaver (http://www.adobe.com/products/dreamweaver/) or iWeb (http://www.apple.com/ilife) (for Mac only).
- You might also want a scanner and CD-R blanks for saving student work.
- In order to make a 30-second video, you will need a low-cost video camera or webcam.
- You will also need an inexpensive dynamic microphone with either a 1/8-inch jack or a 1/4-inch jack and 1/8-inch adapter, which you will plug into the sound card. Budget mics are available for as little as $10, although at that price, the quality will be relatively poor. If you can afford $80 to $100 for a better mic, such as a Shure SM-58 (http://www.shure.com), you will get much better recordings.

Duration: Six to eight class periods to complete all six activities.

Prior Knowledge and Skills: Basic rhythm and composition skills such as note values, form, and meter. In addition, the students need the ability to play a glockenspiel and to use a computer.

Procedure: **Activity 3: Practicing Notes**
1. When students practice reading notes and performing on their instruments, they must learn to think about what the rhythm and pitch are at the same time. Students should evaluate their own performance and should be able to play their composition three times in a row without a mistake before playing it for the teacher.
2. Naturally, the children will be eager to perfect their performance and will look forward to their turn to see themselves on the computer monitor and TV. When my students are able to play their compositions, I give them a red smiley face on their papers and allow them to move on to their next activity.

Evaluation: The students will be able to perform their own compositions on their instruments.

Follow-up: "It's Elementary: A Video Project—Part 4"

Download from www.ti-me.org/TIEMC: None

MENC Standards:	2. Performing on instruments, alone and with others, a varied repertoire of music.
	4. Composing and arranging music within specified guidelines.
	5. Reading and notating music.
	6. Listening to, analyzing, and describing music.
	7. Evaluating music and musical performances.
TI:ME Technology Areas:	2. Music production
	3. Notation software
	5. Multimedia
	6. Productivity tools/information processing/lab management
	7. Web/Internet

It's Elementary: A Video Project—Part 4
ACTIVITY 4: VIDEOTAPE PERFORMANCE
By Maureen Spranza
San Lorenzo Unified School District at Hillside Elementary School, Hayward, California
This article was previously published in the June 2004 issue of *Music Education Technology* magazine,
a property of Penton Media, and is reprinted with the permission of its publisher.
 http://metmagazine.com/mag/elementary/

Grade Level:	Grades K–6
Teacher's Technical Ability:	Advanced
Overall Objective:	The overall objective of this six-part lesson is to create streaming performance videos and original music compositions for publication on the school's website.
Materials/Equipment:	This project is most easily accomplished if you have your own classroom. If you are an itinerant teacher, some aspects might be a bit inconvenient, but the project can still be practical and worthwhile. Here is what you will need.

- Pencils, erasers, and composition-paper templates for everyone in the class. Using a different template for each grade level helps achieve the necessary benchmarks. For instance, in second grade the template can be big enough to allow the children to write their own words. In third grade, I like students to compose a song flute duet, and in fifth grade, we use a template for a 12-bar keyboard blues. In my classroom, the children store their work in a folder, including reference materials with the names of the music symbols we have covered and the symbols' relationships to their instruments.
- A sufficient supply of glockenspiels with mallets, song flutes, recorders, or small keyboards. It might also be helpful to have some music stands. Students can work in pairs or teams, if necessary, to stretch your limited supply of instruments.

- Four desktop computers, complete with USB ports, sound card, speakers, headphones, and at least one computer with a composite-video adapter for connecting your computer to a TV.
- The computers should have Internet access and Finale NotePad freeware (http://www.finalemusic.com). It is also great to have a network server, because that allows students to save their work to a place where you can directly access it from your computer. As we will see, though, there are some caveats regarding younger children having access to a file server.
- You will need Web-publishing software, such as Adobe Macromedia Dreamweaver (http://www.adobe.com/products/dreamweaver/) or iWeb (http://www.apple.com/ilife) (for Mac only).
- You might also want a scanner and CD-R blanks for saving student work.
- In order to make a 30-second video, you will need a low-cost video camera or webcam.
- You will also need an inexpensive dynamic microphone with either a 1/8-inch jack or a 1/4-inch jack and 1/8-inch adapter, which you will plug into the sound card. Budget mics are available for as little as $10, although at that price, the quality will be relatively poor. If you can afford $80 to $100 for a better mic, such as a Shure SM-58 (http://www.shure.com), you will get much better recordings.

Duration: Six to eight class periods to complete all six activities.

Prior Knowledge and Skills: Basic rhythm and composition skills such as note values, form, and meter. In addition, the students need the ability to play a glockenspiel and to use a computer.

Procedure:

Activity 4: Videotape Performance

1. The next activity involves having the students perform for the class and recording the performances with a video camera, if you have one. Of course, this activity is also an opportunity to teach proper audience behavior during a performance.
2. It is helpful to rotate jobs. Have one child aim the camera at the performers and say, "Lights, camera, action," while another child is at the computer, starting and stopping the recording and saving the file. Instruct the performer to say, "Hi, my name is [student's name], and I am playing my composition [title]." Keep the performances short—no longer than 30 seconds—and save the image as a compressed .avi file to keep the file size down.
   a. If you do not have a camera and would like to record audio only, please see many of the lessons in this book that focus on how to record audio with young students. If the files are going to be sent or stored on the Internet, you should save them as .mp3 files, which will save a lot of space and downloading time. If file storage and download time are not factors, you can use .wav or .aiff files.

Evaluation: The students will record themselves performing their compositions.

Follow-up: "It's Elementary: A Video Project—Part 5"

Download from www.ti-me.org/TIEMC: None

MENC Standards:	2. Performing on instruments, alone and with others, a varied repertoire of music.
	4. Composing and arranging music within specified guidelines.
	5. Reading and notating music.
	6. Listening to, analyzing, and describing music.
	7. Evaluating music and musical performances.
TI:ME Technology Areas:	2. Music production
	3. Notation software
	5. Multimedia
	6. Productivity tools/information processing/lab management
	7. Web/Internet

It's Elementary: A Video Project—Part 5
ACTIVITY 5: EVALUATING MUSIC AND PERFORMANCE
By Maureen Spranza
San Lorenzo Unified School District at Hillside Elementary School, Hayward, California

This article was previously published in the June 2004 issue of *Music Education Technology* magazine, a property of Penton Media, and is reprinted with the permission of its publisher.
 http://metmagazine.com/mag/elementary/

Grade Level: Grades K–6

Teacher's Technical Ability: Advanced

Overall Objective: The overall objective of this six-part lesson is to create streaming performance videos and original music compositions for publication on the school's website.

Materials/Equipment: This project is most easily accomplished if you have your own classroom. If you are an itinerant teacher, some aspects might be a bit inconvenient, but the project can still be practical and worthwhile. Here is what you will need.

- Pencils, erasers, and composition-paper templates for everyone in the class. Using a different template for each grade level helps achieve the necessary benchmarks. For instance, in second grade the template can be big enough to allow the children to write their own words. In third grade, I like students to compose a song flute duet, and in fifth grade, we use a template for a 12-bar keyboard blues. In my classroom, the children store their work in a folder, including reference materials with the names of the music symbols we have covered and the symbols' relationships to their instruments.
- A sufficient supply of glockenspiels with mallets, song flutes, recorders, or small keyboards. It might also be helpful to have some music stands. Students can work in pairs or teams, if necessary, to stretch your limited supply of instruments.

- Four desktop computers, complete with USB ports, sound card, speakers, headphones, and at least one computer with a composite-video adapter for connecting your computer to a TV.
- The computers should have Internet access and Finale NotePad freeware (http://www.finalemusic.com). It is also great to have a network server, because that allows students to save their work to a place where you can directly access it from your computer. As we will see, though, there are some caveats regarding younger children having access to a file server.
- You will need Web-publishing software, such as Adobe Macromedia Dreamweaver (http://www.adobe.com/products/dreamweaver/) or iWeb (http://www.apple.com/ilife) (for Mac only).
- You might also want a scanner and CD-R blanks for saving student work.
- In order to make a 30-second video, you will need a low-cost video camera or webcam.
- You will also need an inexpensive dynamic microphone with either a 1/8-inch jack or a 1/4-inch jack and 1/8-inch adapter, which you will plug into the sound card. Budget mics are available for as little as $10, although at that price, the quality will be relatively poor. If you can afford $80 to $100 for a better mic, such as a Shure SM-58 (http://www.shure.com), you will get much better recordings.

Duration: Six to eight class periods to complete all six activities.

Prior Knowledge and Skills: Basic rhythm and composition skills such as note values, form, and meter. In addition, the students need the ability to play a glockenspiel and to use a computer.

Procedure: **Activity 5: Evaluating Music and Performance**
1. After a student performs for the camera, it's time for audience members to give feedback. The children in the audience raise their hands, and the performer selects among them. The performer then asks the selected student questions like, "What did you like?" and "What could have been better?"
2. Next, the class can view the videos on the computer using Microsoft's Windows Media Player (http://www.microsoft.com/windows/windowsmedia), Apple's QuickTime (http://www.apple.com/quicktime/download), Apple's iMovie (http://www.apple.com/ilife/imovie/), or whatever video-playback software you have, using them to stimulate a discussion of the final "product." For the final assessment, you can use a scoring rubric (see "Evaluation," below).
3. This project can extend beyond the subject of music. For example, teachers at any level can create inexpensive streaming video of their students doing oral language activities.

Evaluation: This scoring rubric is designed to assist in assessing the music and performance listening exercises. In the following example, we are evaluating K–2 students, as indicated by the use of glockenspiels. This rubric can also be found on the TI:ME website.

Points	3	2	1
Paper and Computer	Uses half notes or rests, quarter notes or rests, eighth notes or rests	Only a few errors	Symbols are not used consistently
	Correct notes: do, mi sol, la (C, E, G, A)	1–2 errors	3–4 errors
	Two beats in the measure (meter), with correct bar lines	1–2 errors	3–4 errors
	Prosodic (music represents title)	Representation can be re-created another day	Better choices might have been made
Glocken-spiel Video	Excellent rhythms, steady beat	Good rhythms, generally steady beat	Rhythms and beat are unsteady
	Correct notes/pitches	1–2 errors	3–4 errors
	Timbre is excellent, mallets held correctly	Tone is generally good	Tone is not ringing
	Head up and shoulders erect	Good position and posture	Marginally acceptable position and posture
Discussion	Emphasizes extra musical aspects of the composition	References how good the performance was technically, as well as how musical it was	Says, "I liked it" when he or she didn't
	Always uses correct terminology rather than general vocabulary terms	Uses correct terminology	Uses incorrect terminology
	Students evaluate whether they remained quiet, seated with legs and arms still, with their eyes watching and their ears listening, and reserved their applause	Demonstrated appropriate behavior	Evaluated whether they demonstrated questionable behaviors such as tapping feet, shouting, getting up, talking, humming along

When I evaluate fifth graders, I use the following rubric (see Fig. 2.22), which can also be found on the TI:ME website.

Name_____ Classroom Teacher_____

5th Grade Music
Final Composition Project
Writing

	4	3	2	1	Self-Score	Teacher Score
Time Signature	Time signature used properly	Time signature used properly	Time signature used properly	No time signature		
Rhythms	All rhythms from checklist are used	Most rhythms from checklist are used	Some rhythms from checklist are used	Hardly any rhythms from checklist are used		
Notes	Sharps and flats are used	Sharps and flats are used	Notes are unplayable by you	Notes are unplayable by you		
Articulation	Staccato and legato are used	Staccato and legato are used	Staccato or legato is used	Neither staccato nor legato are used		
Harmony	I, IV, and V chords are used	I and IV or I and V chords are used	I chord is used	No chords are used		
Tempo	Song is labeled with a tempo(s)	Song is labeled with a tempo	No tempo marking	No tempo marking		
Dynamics	Dynamic markings are used	Dynamic markings are used	No dynamic markings are used	No dynamic markings are used		
Technique	Ostinato, canon, augmentation, diminution are used	Ostinato, canon, augmentation, diminution are used	Some additional techniques are used	No additional techniques are used		

Performance Video

	4	3	2	1	Student Score	Teacher Score
Rhythm and Beat	Excellent rhythms, steady beat	Excellent rhythms, steady beat	Good rhythms, generally steady beat	Rhythms and beat are unsteady		
Notes	Correct notes/pitches	Correct notes/pitches	1–2 errors	3–4 errors		
Timbre/Tone/Sound	Timbre is excellent, hands held correctly	Timbre is excellent, hands held correctly	Tone is generally good	Tone is not ringing		
Posture	Head is up and shoulders are erect	Head is up and shoulders are erect	Good position and posture	Marginally acceptable posture and position		

Fig. 2.22: Fifth grade evaluation rubric that can be found on the TI:ME website.

Follow-up: "It's Elementary: A Video Project—Part 6"

Download from   • "Elementary_Part5.pdf"
www.ti-me.org/TIEMC: • "5th_rubric.pdf"

MENC Standards:	2. Performing on instruments, alone and with others, a varied repertoire of music.
	4. Composing and arranging music within specified guidelines.
	5. Reading and notating music.
	6. Listening to, analyzing, and describing music.
	7. Evaluating music and musical performances.
TI:ME Technology Areas:	2. Music production
	3. Notation software
	5. Multimedia
	6. Productivity tools/information processing/lab management
	7. Web/Internet

It's Elementary: A Video Project—Part 6
ACTIVITY 6: WEB PAGE
By Maureen Spranza
San Lorenzo Unified School District at Hillside Elementary School, Hayward, California

This article was previously published in the June 2004 issue of *Music Education Technology* magazine, a property of Penton Media, and is reprinted with the permission of its publisher.
http://metmagazine.com/mag/elementary/

Grade Level:	Grades K–6
Teacher's Technical Ability:	Advanced
Overall Objective:	The overall objective of this six-part lesson is to create streaming performance videos and original music compositions for publication on the school's website.
Materials/Equipment:	This project is most easily accomplished if you have your own classroom. If you are an itinerant teacher, some aspects might be a bit inconvenient, but the project can still be practical and worthwhile. Here is what you will need.

- Pencils, erasers, and composition-paper templates for everyone in the class. Using a different template for each grade level helps achieve the necessary benchmarks. For instance, in second grade the template can be big enough to allow the children to write their own words. In third grade, I like students to compose a song flute duet, and in fifth grade, we use a template for a 12-bar keyboard blues. In my classroom, the children store their work in a folder, including reference materials with the names of the music symbols we have covered and the symbols' relationships to their instruments.
- A sufficient supply of glockenspiels with mallets, song flutes, recorders, or small keyboards. It might also be helpful to have some music stands. Students can work in pairs or teams, if necessary, to stretch your limited supply of instruments.

- Four desktop computers, complete with USB ports, sound card, speakers, headphones, and at least one computer with a composite-video adapter for connecting your computer to a TV.
- The computers should have Internet access and Finale NotePad freeware (http://www.finalemusic.com). It is also great to have a network server, because that allows students to save their work to a place where you can directly access it from your computer. As we will see, though, there are some caveats regarding younger children having access to a file server.
- You will need Web-publishing software, such as Adobe Macromedia Dreamweaver (http://www.adobe.com/products/dreamweaver/) or iWeb (http://www.apple.com/ilife) (for Mac only).
- You might also want a scanner and CD-R blanks for saving student work.
- In order to make a 30-second video, you will need a low-cost video camera or webcam.
- You will also need an inexpensive dynamic microphone with either a 1/8-inch jack or a 1/4-inch jack and 1/8-inch adapter, which you will plug into the sound card. Budget mics are available for as little as $10, although at that price, the quality will be relatively poor. If you can afford $80 to $100 for a better mic, such as a Shure SM-58 (http://www.shure.com), you will get much better recordings.

Duration: Six to eight class periods to complete all six activities.

Prior Knowledge and Skills: Basic rhythm and composition skills such as note values, form, and meter. In addition, the students need the ability to play a glockenspiel and to use a computer.

Procedure:

Activity 6: Web Page

1. The Web is a great place for children to display their videos and music compositions. Children can view and listen to each other's work, and parents can see and hear exactly what their child is doing in music class. Families with home computers can download, view, and even experiment with their child's work at home, using widely available (and often free) software. This is also an opportunity to see the work of other children. Teachers can get lesson ideas by seeing what someone else is doing.
    a. Before we get further into this, it is important to note that this activity is not appropriate for everyone, and it involves a number of special considerations regarding privacy and security. It might be worthwhile to discuss the project in advance with some other parents you consider to be representative of the group, so that you can account for possible objections while you are still in the planning stages.
    b. For starters, before you can publish student work and student video images to the Web, you will need parents to sign a permission slip, such as a "Student Work Release Form: Internet Web Project Publishing." Preface this permission slip with a letter to the parents describing your project and offering instructions on how to view their child's work online. You need permission to post the child's original composition, the actual music performance (a separate issue from the composition), and especially the child's image in the video.
    c. One way to help ensure security and privacy is to set up a password-protected area on the website where the videos, in particular, can be placed. This is a smart move even if nobody requests it. Even with this precaution, though, some parents will not want videos of their children posted to the Internet.

Privacy and personal safety are valid reasons for such a decision, so if that is the response you get, you will just have to accept it and modify the activity. For example, if parents object only to posting the videos, you could ask permission to post just the Finale NotePad files and an audio recording of the music, without images.

2. Assuming the parents approve and the permission slips are returned, add the Finale NotePad files and the video files to the school website in front of the class. Your students will gain experience by watching this process, and the more capable older students might even learn to publish the files themselves. (Older students can easily learn this skill, but it can be a difficult challenge for younger students.)

3. It is important to realize that although broadband Internet connections are becoming commonplace, many parents probably still do not have broadband service. Therefore, it is wise to provide downloadable files in addition to or instead of streaming video. Use a format that can be played on both Macintosh and Windows computers. Windows Media is an excellent format because the quality is good and players for Macintosh, Windows, Linux, Palm, and other operating systems can be downloaded free from Microsoft.

Evaluation: The students will view and/or listen to their compositions on the school's website.

Follow-up: You can find virtually endless ways to use technology to enhance your teaching methods. For example, you can also have the students create CD covers using a draw, paint, or photo-editing program, which addresses MENC Standard 8 (understanding relationships between music, the other arts, and disciplines outside the arts).

A more elaborate idea that addresses MENC standards 6 and 9 is a collaborative research and presentation project on music from a country of the student's choice. This could be done using the Web and a presentation program such as Microsoft PowerPoint (http://office.microsoft.com/en-us/powerpoint/default.aspx) or Apple Keynote (http://www.apple.com/iwork/keynote/). I also recommend incorporating the Big6 information-literacy techniques (http://www.big6.com/showarticle.php?id=107). Project-based learning (PBL) works. As you might expect, it takes many hours to plan and prepare projects and well-organized Web pages. Furthermore, the success of an Internet-based project depends on the age of the students, the number of students involved, and the degree to which parents and others in the community can access the Internet. However, the PBL approach offers tremendous learning potential for teachers and students alike, and the technology required is rapidly becoming mainstream. Start planning now and watch your students reach new levels of achievement—and have fun doing it.

**Download from
www.ti-me.org/TIEMC:** None

PART 3

TECHNOLOGY-ENHANCED LESSON PLANS THAT EMPHASIZE LISTENING TO MUSIC, AND THE INTER- AND INTRA- RELATIONSHIPS* IN MUSIC, BY ADDRESSING THE MENC STANDARDS 6, 7, 8, AND 9:

6. **Listening to, analyzing, and describing music.**
7. **Evaluating music and music performances.**
8. **Understanding relationships between music, the other arts, and disciplines outside the arts.**
9. **Understanding music in relation to history and culture.**

*"Inter" meaning what music means to the students, and "intra" meaning how the students relate to music culturally and historically.

| MENC Standards: | 2. Performing on instruments, alone and with others, a varied repertoire of music. |
| | 6. Listening to, analyzing, and describing music. |

TI:ME Technology Areas:	2. Music production
	4. Instructional music software
	5. Multimedia
	6. Productivity tools/information processing/lab management

Tapping a Steady Beat
By Steven Estrella
Shearspire, Inc.

Grade Level:	K–6
Teacher's Technical Ability:	Intermediate
Objective:	At the conclusion of this lesson, students will be able to tap a steady beat in response to music played at 60 beats per minute, 90 beats per minute, and 120 beats per minute.
Materials/Equipment:	• MIDI files of Bach Inventions 4, 8, and 13 (see "Download from www.ti-me.org/TIEMC").
	• Microphone.
	• Amplifier.
	• Steady beat interactive exercises that are available at the McGraw-Hill online learning site for the *Music First!* textbook. You can find them at: http://www.mhhe.com/musicfirst5. Click "Student edition," then "Activities," then "Activity 3.1: Tapping a Steady Beat."
Duration:	
	40 minutes
Prior Knowledge and Skills:	Students need not have any special skills or knowledge. This will be a largely kinesthetic activity.
Procedure:	

1. To prepare for this lesson, the teacher must download MIDI files of Bach Inventions 4, 8, and 13 (see "Download from www.ti-me.org/TIEMC").
2. These pieces must then be loaded into music production software and modified as needed to ensure no changes in tempo. Bach Invention 4 should play at 60 bpm throughout, Invention 13 should play at 90 bpm, and Invention 8 should play at 120 bpm.
3. First ten minutes:
   Ask for a volunteer from among the students. Turn on the microphone and amplifier and ask the student to put the mic up to his or her heart. For younger students, you may have to direct them to the left side of the chest. Use this demonstration to discuss the concept of pulse with your students. Ask them to identify other regular pulses in nature (breathing, tides, rising and setting of the sun, etc.).

4. Next five minutes:
   Walk across the room at a slow and steady pace of about 60 steps per minute (one each second). Have the class clap their hands on each footfall. Then ask the class to continue clapping the pulse even after you stop walking. Discuss the aesthetic effect of tapping a slow and steady beat. Does it remind you of walking or relaxed breathing?

5. Next five minutes:
   Walk across the room at a fast and steady pace of about 120 steps per minute (two each second). Again, have the class clap on each footfall. Discuss the aesthetic effect of the faster tempo and relate it to the way the heart races after running.

6. Next five minutes:
   a. Next, divide the class into teams labeled the "Macros" and the "Micros." Walk across the room at 60 steps per minute and ask the Macros to clap once on each footfall. Ask the Micros to snap two times per footfall.
   b. Repeat the example and have the Micros snap three times per footfall. Explain that in most music, you can hear big beats (the claps) and little beats (the snaps). The big beats are sometimes divided into two little beats and sometimes into three little beats depending on the nature of the music.

7. Next five minutes:
   a. Have your computer and sequencer ready with Bach Invention 4.
   b. Play it at a steady 60 bpm. Ask students to move forward on each big beat by one step and then backward on the next big beat. This simple movement activity helps to cement steady beat understanding by involving the thighs and other large muscle groups. When students are able to coordinate the steady beat in this way, ask them to snap three times per big beat. Students should be physically engaged so that beat and meter are internalized.

8. Next ten minutes:
   Repeat this activity with Bach Invention 13 at 90 bpm and Bach Invention 8 at 120 bpm, but have the students snap only twice during each big beat for these two works.

9. End the class by sending the students home with instructions to practice this activity during the week. Evaluation will take place one week later in the computer lab.

Evaluation: One week after the lesson, schedule your class for time in the computer lab. Load activity 3.1 from chapter 3 of *Music First!* online learning center found at: http://www.mhhe.com/musicfirst. Have the *Music First!* screen on each computer when students arrive. Use the teacher station and video projector to demonstrate how the application works. Have students begin with Bach Invention 4 and have them tap the beat on the shift key of the keyboard. The software measures the students' accuracy and provides a score for steady beat. Go around to each station and record each student's score on Bach Invention 4 (60 bpm). Then have the students work on the other two inventions (No. 13 at 90 bpm and No. 8 at 120 bpm). Record all scores in a spreadsheet and use this information to individualize instruction as needed to ensure all students learn the vital skill of steady beat.

Follow-up: A logical follow-up lesson to this one would introduce duple and triple meter.

Items to Be Purchased: The teacher will need a computer with notation and/or music production software, a Web browser with the Flash plug-in installed, and access to the Internet.

Download from
www.ti-me.org/TIEMC:
- "Bach_Invent4.mid"
- "Bach_Invent8.mid"
- "Bach_Invent13.mid"

MENC Standards:	1. Singing, alone and with others, a varied repertoire of music.
	2. Performing on instruments, alone and with others, a varied repertoire of music.
	6. Listening to, analyzing, and describing music.
	7. Evaluating music and musical performances.
TI:ME Technology Areas:	5. Multimedia
	7. Web/Internet

Teaching Tempo

By Amy M. Burns

Far Hills Country Day School, Far Hills, New Jersey

This article was previously published in the September 2005 issue of *Music Education Technology* magazine, a property of Penton Media, and is reprinted with the permission of its publisher.

http://metmagazine.com/lessonplan/teaching_tempo/

Grade Level: Grade 1

Teacher's Technical Ability: Novice

Objective: When my first graders are studying a unit about tempo, we perform various activities involving singing, moving, listening, and performing on instruments. This lesson's objective is for the students to be able to identify, sing, perform, and move to the tempos of *adagio*, *moderato*, and *presto*. This lesson is spread over several music classes. At the conclusion of the unit, I assess their knowledge of the three terms.

Materials/Equipment:
- "*Adagio*," "*Moderato*," and "*Presto*" signs.
- Pictures of a turtle, representing *adagio*; a person walking, representing *moderato*; and a bee, representing *presto*.
- The scavenger hunt worksheet (see "Files on the Website"), on which the students answer questions about tempo.
- The lyrics and melody of the song "I Have a Car," or a similar favorite song of the students.
- Listening samples of music at various tempos, preferably including Rimsky-Korsakov's "Flight of the Bumble Bee" and Saint-Saëns's "The Swan."
- A multi-station computer lab with Web access—if you have only one computer, its display output should be hooked to a big-screen TV or an LCD projector with a screen.
- San Francisco Symphony Kids website: http://www.sfskids.org/templates/musicLabF.asp?pageid=11.

Duration: Three class periods

Prior Knowledge and Skills: This lesson introduces the concept of tempo, so no prior knowledge is necessary.

Procedure: **First music class**

1. Begin the first section of the lesson by introducing the tempo or speed of the music by listening to various songs and tapping the steady beat.
2. Discuss how the beat changed from fast to slow.
3. As a visual aid, show pictures of animals that move quickly and slowly and identify their speed in musical terms, introducing *presto* for very fast movement and *adagio* for very slow movement.
4. As an aural example, play Rimsky-Korsakov's "Flight of the Bumblebee," and have the students describe the tempo as fast/*presto*.
5. Then have the students move like bees to "Flight of the Bumblebee." Next, play Saint-Saëns's "The Swan" and have the students describe the tempo as slow/*adagio*.
6. Have the students move like turtles to "The Swan." After that, introduce the "Bees and Turtles" game: when you play music that is *presto*, the students move like bees; when you play music that is *adagio*, they move like turtles.

Second music class

1. Review the ideas of *presto* and *adagio* through pictures and movement.
2. When the review is completed, you can move on to teaching *moderato*. Sing "I Have a Car," or a similar popular children's song and identify a new tempo that is not too fast and not too slow as medium/*moderato*.
3. Then have the students sing the song as though the car were running out of gas. Identify the tempo as *adagio*.
4. After that, have the students sing the song as though the car were trying to win a race. Identify the tempo as *presto*.
5. To complete that part of the lesson, have the students perform *presto*, *moderato*, and *adagio* rhythms with egg shakers, changing tempo along with the music.

Third music class

1. This class introduces the technology portion of the lesson.
2. Sign out a time for the students to meet you in the school's computer lab; the lab at my school is equipped with 19 iMac computers containing software, CD-ROMs, and headphones, and it has Internet access, which is needed for this lesson.
3. Prepare the lab ahead of time by having the music lab section of the San Francisco Symphony's SFS Kids Fun with Music website (http://www.sfskids.org/templates/ musicLabF.asp?pageid=11) already on the computer screens.
4. Click on the "Tempo" link, then click on the metronome to get started (see Fig. 3.1). This is an excellent website where young students can learn and apply basic musical skills.
5. Hand out the scavenger hunt worksheet (see "Download from www.ti-me.org/TIEMC"), and explain to the students that they will use the website to find the items on the sheet. The worksheet and website reinforce the unit and the students' recall about tempo.

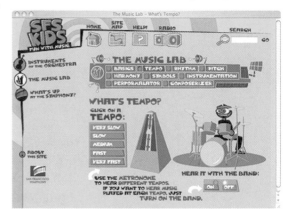

Fig. 3.1: http://www.sfskids.org.

Level of Achievement	Identifying the Difference Between Tempos	Use of Terminology
Excellent	Student can hear and identify the difference when the drummer plays adagio, moderato, and presto.	Student can identify and define the terms adagio, moderato, and presto with no assistance from the teacher.
Good	Student can hear and identify the difference when the drummer plays adagio and presto but cannot comprehend moderato.	Student can identify and define the terms adagio, moderato, and presto with little assistance from the teacher.
Fair	Student can hear the difference when the drummer plays adagio, moderato, and presto but cannot identify them.	Student can identify and define the terms adagio and presto but does not comprehend moderato.
Novice	Student can neither hear nor identify the difference when the drummer plays adagio, moderato, and presto.	Student does not comprehend the terms adagio, moderato, and presto.

Fig. 3.2: Rubric.

Evaluation: This lesson will produce various lessons of achievements. The ideal outcome is that the students successfully identify the difference between *adagio, moderato,* and *presto.* The rubric (see Fig. 3.2) shows various examples of levels of achievement.

Follow-up: This lesson can be followed up with the students performing various tempos on classroom percussion instruments.

Items to Be Purchased: If you have access to a computer lab with the Internet, then you will not need to purchase anything for this lesson. If you are using one computer in your classroom with Internet access, then there are no additional materials needed to make this lesson possible. You might need to purchase an adapter that will let your computer screen project to a TV. However, please ask around school because it is likely that an adapter might be found elsewhere in the school. The only extra step you might need to take is to sign out the TV, projection screen, or Smart Board in advance.

Download from www.ti-me.org/TIEMC: "Tempo_Worksheet.pdf"

MENC Standards: K–4 Standard: 6. Listening to, analyzing, and describing music.
Pre-K Standard: 3. Responding to music.

TI:ME Technology Areas: 5. Multimedia

Music and Movement for Kindergartners
By Amy M. Burns
Far Hills Country Day School, Far Hills, New Jersey

Grade Level: Kindergarten (this lesson also works well with pre-Kindergarten)

Teacher's Technical Ability: Novice

Objective: The students will move and respond to music.

Materials/Equipment:
- CD player.
- Musical selection to which the students will perform the guided movements.
- PowerPoint of the stick figure movements that the students will imitate in this lesson (see "Download from www.ti-me.org/TIEMC").
- Computer with Microsoft's PowerPoint software or Apple's Keynote, projected onto a screen with an LCD projector, or onto a TV.

Duration: 15 minutes

Prior Knowledge and Skills: This lesson uses the movements that correlate with MENC's *SoundPlay: Understanding Music through Creative Movement* (2000); however the book is not necessary for this lesson. These movements are walking, running, hopping, jumping, skipping, crawling, shaking, twisting, freezing, and sitting.

Procedure:
1. Review each movement with the students in an open space.
2. Choose a musical selection that will enhance the movements.
3. Turn on the projector and load the PowerPoint (see "Download from www.ti-me.org/TIEMC").
4. Have the students "freeze" until you begin the music and PowerPoint.
5. Have the students move to the guided movements in the PowerPoint as you run the PowerPoint from the computer. If you have a remote control to run the PowerPoint, then feel free to perform the movements along with the students.

Evaluation: The students move and respond to the music by following the guided movements on the PowerPoint.

Follow-up: To follow up this lesson, you can have the students create and improvise their own movements individually and in groups.

Items to Be Purchased: If you have a computer in your room that contains Microsoft's PowerPoint or Apple's Keynote, then you will only need to acquire the school's LCD projector and screen, or an adapter that projects onto a TV screen.

Download from www.ti-me.org/TIEMC: "Music_and_Movement.ppt"

MENC Standards:	1. Singing, alone and with others, a varied repertoire of music.
	2. Performing on instruments, alone and with others, a varied repertoire of music.
	6. Listening to, analyzing, and describing music.
	7. Evaluating music and musical performances.
TI:ME Technology Areas:	1. Electronic instruments

Upward and Downward Motion

By Kelly Conlon

Anna McCabe Elementary School, Smithfield, Rhode Island

Grade Level: Grade 1

Teacher's Technical Ability: Novice

Objective:
1. Student will be able to identify upward and downward motion (higher and lower) through singing.
2. Students will be able to identify upward and downward motion by creating movements to demonstrate higher and lower.
3. Students will demonstrate upward and downward motion by playing the xylophone and electronic keyboard.

Materials/Equipment:
- Silver Burdett's *The Music Connection*, Grade 1, Teacher Edition.
- Silver Burdett's *The Music Connection*, Grade 1, Student Edition.
- Silver Burdett's *The Music Connection*, Grade 1, CD.
- CD player.
- Xylophone with a mallet.
- Electronic keyboard.

Duration: 40 minutes

Prior Knowledge and Skills:
1. Students understand the concept of steady beat.
2. Students can recognize the changes in pitch.
3. Students have basic knowledge of the different sounds of instruments.
4. Student can play the xylophone.

Procedure:
1. Introduce lesson (up/downward) by playing the xylophone and asking students to identify what they hear. (Answer: different sounds.)
2. Introduce the concept of upward/downward and show that as each note is played, it will sound either higher or lower. (As I play upward, I move my hand in an upward motion, etc.)
3. Students will use their hands to demonstrate whether they hear the notes moving upward or downward.
4. Students will practice playing upward and downward on xylophone.

5. Introduce the song "Ebeneezer Sneezer" (see "Items to Be Purchased") and teach the children to sing it. (The melody moves up and down a major scale.)
6. Children will stand and create body movements to identify the upward and downward motions in the song.
7. Children will take turns playing upward/downward on the keyboard as their classmates decide whether they hear upward or downward motion.
8. Review with the class the difference between a flute and a violin.
9. Demonstrate to children that although the sound of the instrument changes, both instruments can still play upward and downward.
10. Continue to have children play up/downward on the keyboard while classmates guess which direction is being played (up or down) and which instrument they hear (flute or violin).

Evaluation:

1. At the end of this lesson, I will assess my students understanding of upward and downward motion by observing them. The final step in this lesson is for each student to play up/down on the keyboard and be able to identify which they are playing.
2. At the end of this unit, students will be given a listening test and will need to identify upward and downward motion.

Follow-up:

A possible follow-up lesson would be to introduce the woodwind family of instruments. Students would again play upward and downward on the keyboard, but in addition, they would need to identify which woodwind instrument they heard.

Items to Be Purchased:

The items required for this lesson are xylophones, Silver Burdett's *The Music Connection* series (if you do not have this series, the song "Ebeneezer Sneezer" can be previewed on http://www.sheetmusicdigital.com/Soleroitem.asp?ID=SH00283356), and an electronic keyboard.

Download from www.ti-me.org/TIEMC:

None

MENC Standards:	1. Singing, alone and with others, a varied repertoire of music.
	6. Listening to, analyzing, and describing music.
TI:ME Technology Areas:	4. Instructional music software

Identifying Pitch

By Amy M. Burns
Far Hills Country Day School, Far Hills, New Jersey

Grade Level:	K–2
Teacher's Technical Ability:	Novice
Objective:	The students will identify when the pitch is the same or different. In addition, they will identify when the pitch goes higher, lower, and/or stays the same.
Materials/Equipment:	• Slide whistle. • "I Can Slide" song (see "Download from www.ti-me.org/TIEMC"). • Harmonic Vision's Music Ace 1: Lesson 3 or Music Ace Maestro: Lesson 4, and a computer hooked to a TV, Smart Board, or LCD projector and screen.
Duration:	1–2 class periods (30 minutes each)
Prior Knowledge and Skills:	The students need to feel comfortable singing and moving to music.

I Can Slide

Fig. 3.3: The song "I Can Slide."

Procedure:	1. Introduce the song "I Can Slide" (see Fig. 3.3 and "Download from www.ti-me.org/TIEMC"). 2. Echo-sing the song. 3. Sing the song together, emphasizing the slide at the end of the song. 4. Demonstrate how to slide and have the students slide while they sing the song. 5. Take out your slide whistle and have the students move up and down while you play high and low. 6. Explain to the students that pitch (or sound) can move high, low, or stay the same. 7. Play the slide whistle again and have the students move while you play high, low, and stay the same.

8. You can further reinforce this concept by having the students make a siren noise and have them move to musical excerpts that include pitches that move from low to high and vice versa.

9. During the next class, we review the concept of high pitches, low pitches, pitches that stay the same, and moving from low to high and high to low.

10. To assess how the students comprehend the concept of pitch, have the students sit around the TV, Smart Board, or screen that is hooked to the computer.

11. Launch Harmonic Vision's Music Ace 1: Lesson 3 or Music Ace Maestro: Lesson 4.

12. Have the students accomplish Music Ace 1: Lesson 3 or Music Ace Maestro: Lesson 4, sections 1, 2, and 3:

   a. Section 1 quizzes the students on identifying pitch as same or different.

   b. Section 2 quizzes the students on identifying if one pitch is higher, lower, or the same as the other pitch.

   c. Section 3 gives the students excellent visual and audio on how the slider will move up to produce a higher pitch and down to produce a lower pitch.

   d. I leave out sections 4 and 5 because it is about moving the slider to match the pitch. I find that my first and second graders have a difficult time with this.

Evaluation: This lesson can produce various levels of achievement. Therefore, I created this rubric to assist in evaluating the students. If I am using this lesson in a Kindergarten or first grade general music class, I will assess them as a group. If I am using this lesson with second graders in a computer lab, then I will assess them individually.

	Section 1	Section 2
Excellent	The students can successfully identify when the pitches are the same or different without assistance from the teacher.	The students can successfully identify when one pitch is higher, lower, or the same as the other pitch, with no assistance from the teacher.
Good	The students can successfully identify when the pitches are the same or different with little assistance from the teacher.	The students can successfully identify when one pitch is higher lower, or the same as the other pitch, with little assistance from the teacher.
Fair	The students can successfully identify when the pitches are the same or different with much assistance from the teacher.	The students can successfully identify when one pitch is higher lower, or the same as the other pitch, with much assistance from the teacher.
Novice	The students cannot identify when the pitches are the same or different, even with assistance from the teacher.	The students cannot identify when one pitch is higher, lower, or the same as the other pitch, even with assistance from the teacher.

Follow-up: This lesson can be followed up with additional movement and singing lessons about pitch.

Items to Be Purchased: Harmonic Vision's Music Ace 1 or Music Ace Maestro (http://www.harmonicvision.com) are fairly inexpensive programs when purchased as a single copy. They becomes more expensive when purchased as a 5-pack, 15-pack, 30-pack, or network version thereof. However, if you plan to use one of these programs in the school's computer lab, then the lab packs or network versions are definitely worth the cost.

Download from www.ti-me.org/TIEMC: "I_Can_Slide.pdf"

MENC Standards:	4. Composing and arranging music within specified guidelines.
	5. Reading and notating music.
	6. Listening to, analyzing, and describing music.
TI:ME Technology Areas:	1. Electronic instruments
	2. Music production
	3. Notation software

Can You Fix the Incorrect Pitches?

By Robin Hansen,
Lafayette School, Chatham, New Jersey

Grade Level:	Grade 4
Teacher's Technical Ability:	Advanced
Objective:	The fourth grade general music students will listen to a single-line music sequence of a familiar song that contains incorrect pitches, determine which notes are wrong, and drag them to the correct pitches in both graphic and notation view.
Materials/Equipment:	• Computers with a sequencing program. • Headphones. • MIDI output device such as a keyboard (optional). If you do not want to sequence the musical line, you can use the MIDI files that are provided (see "Download from www.ti-me.org/TIEMC"). • LCD projector (optional).
Duration:	30 minutes
Prior Knowledge and Skills:	Students must have prior knowledge of pitch direction, the songs the teacher uses in the sequence, and how to change pitches in a graphic and notation editor.
Procedure:	1. Before class, the teacher will prepare four single-line sequences of short familiar songs (*i.e.*, "Jingle Bells," "Yankee Doodle," "Happy Birthday," "Merrily We Roll Along," etc.) with several wrong pitches included in each. a. You can also use the MIDI files provided on the TI:ME website (see "Download from www.ti-me.org/TIEMC"). 2. Working in pairs, students will listen to the first example, and while in graphic view will correct the errors by dragging the notes to the correct pitches. (Teacher can demonstrate this on the computer connected to a LCD projector projected onto a screen, if available.) 3. Students may listen to the example with their proposed corrections as often as necessary while they continue to make changes. 4. When the first example is done, the students may go on to example number 2. 5. The same procedure will be used on examples 3 and 4, but these will be corrected in notation view.

Evaluation: Students will be able to self-assess their work by listening to the example as often as necessary. The teacher will circulate and listen to finished examples. If there are students who have not corrected all the wrong notes, then the teacher will play the example as it should sound and the student will go back and fix errors. The teacher may have to guide challenged students through the process.

Follow-up: Follow-up lessons could include using the same songs but altering the rhythms. Corrections should only be made in the graphic editor as this is an ear-training lesson. Advanced music students could use the notation view to edit.

Download from www.ti-me.org/TIEMC: The sequencing files for "Yankee Doodle," "Jingle Bells," "Happy Birthday," and "Merrily We Roll Along," can be found as MIDI (.mid) files on the TI:ME website. The word "Correct" in the file's name means that the correct notes are played in the melody; "Incorrect" means that incorrect notes are played. Since these are MIDI files, they will need to be opened with any sequencing program, such as Cakewalk Sonar Home Studio, Apple's GarageBand, or MOTU's Digital Performer.
- "Yankee_Doodle_Correct.mid"
- "Yankee_Doodle_Incorrect.mid"
- "Jingle_Bells_Correct.mid"
- "Jingle_Bells_Incorrect.mid"
- "Happy_Birthday_Correct.mid"
- "Happy_Birthday_Incorrect.mid"
- "Merrily_We_Roll_Along_Correct.mid"
- "Merrily_We_Roll_Along_Incorrect.mid"

Instrument Concentration Game for Early Childhood/Elementary

By Amy M. Burns
Far Hills Country Day School, Far Hills, New Jersey

Grade Level:	Pre-K–4
Teacher's Technical Ability:	Novice
Objective:	The students will be able to correctly identify orchestral musical instruments through sight and sound. In addition, they will be able to match the instruments with their sounds.
Materials/Equipment:	• Computer with Internet access projected onto a TV or a projection screen. • Smart Board (which requires an adapter that runs from your computer into the screen).

This lesson requires your computer to produce adequate sound so that you and your students hear the sound excerpts. Alternatively, this lesson can be done in a computer lab. The website that you will be using is the New York Philharmonic Kidzone (http://www.nyphilkids.org/games).

Duration:	15 minutes
Prior Knowledge and Skills:	This lesson coordinates with a unit on musical instruments and their sounds. The only prior knowledge necessary is knowledge of the names of and ability to visually recognize the instruments.
Procedure:	1. Before class, open an Internet browser. 2. Type in this address: http://www.nyphilkids.org/games. This is the site for the New York Philharmonic Kidzone. 3. Click on "Music Match Instruments." 4. Choose the level to play. There are three levels. The higher the level, the more choices your students will have to match. If this is a first grade class, level 1 or 2 would be appropriate (see Fig. 3.4). 5. When the students walk into the room, have them sit down facing the TV (or projection screen or the Smart Board screen). They will see the concentration game up on screen. 6. Ask them if they have ever played "Concentration" or other matching game before. 7. Explain to them that they will be finding the match of the first card that they flip. For example, if they flip over the clarinet card, then they will need to find the other clarinet card.

120

8. Choose a student to go to the computer, and by using the computer's mouse, flip over the first card. The card will play an excellent audio excerpt of that instrument.

9. The student then flips over another card to see if it was the match. The students will know if it matched through visual and audio cues.

10. Choose a student for each turn. Play until all of the cards are flipped over. If all of the students have not had a turn, start a new game and play until everyone has had a turn.

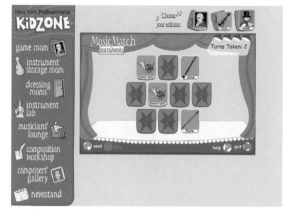

Fig. 3.4: Young students love the "Music Match Instruments" game from the New York Philharmonic KidZone site.

11. My students love playing this game! At the end of the game, a score appears, which makes my kids shout for joy. I once had a group of kindergartners jump up and down in excitement each time a student successfully matched two instruments.

Evaluation: The students will be able to name correctly the orchestral instruments through sight and sound. The more you play the game, the better the students will become at naming the instruments through their pictures and their audio excerpts. The following rubric has been made to clarify assessment. The teacher can choose whether to assess the student individually or the class as a whole.

	Identifying instrument by sight and sound
Excellent	The student can name the instrument by sight and sound with no assistance from the teacher.
Good	The student can name the instrument by sight and sound with some assistance from the teacher.
Fair	The student can name the instrument by sight and sound with much assistance from the teacher.
Novice	The student cannot name the instrument by sight and sound even with assistance from the teacher.

For younger students (pre-K–Kindergarten), the experience of seeing and hearing the sounds of the instruments will be the result, as opposed to being able to name all of the instruments and identify all of their sounds.

Follow-up: There are various ways to follow up this lesson. The teacher could play "Instrument Bingo" to reinforce the concepts of this lesson. The teacher could give pictures of the instruments to young students and arrange the students in the orchestral seating positions. Then the teacher could choose one student to be the conductor. The teacher could play any orchestral piece that features instrumental families (like Karl MacDonald's *Children Symphony 1st Movement*, or Benjamin Britten's *The Young Person's Guide to the Symphony*) and have the students hold up their instruments' pictures when they hear their instruments performing.

Items to Be Purchased: If you have a computer in your classroom with Internet access, then no additional materials are needed. However, you might need to purchase an adapter for projecting your computer screen onto a TV. Please check your school inventory for an adapter before purchasing. To ensure that you'll have the equipment you need for your class period, you also may want to consider signing out the equipment in advance.

Download from www.ti-me.org/TIEMC: None

MENC Standards:	6. Listening to, analyzing, and describing music.
	8. Understanding relationships between music, the other arts, and disciplines outside the arts.
	9. Understanding music in relation to history and culture.
TI:ME Technology Areas:	5. Multimedia
	7. Web/Internet

Benjamin Franklin and the Glass Armonica
By Christine Dunleavy
Winslow Township Elementary School #5, Winslow Township, New Jersey

Grade Level: Grade 5

Teacher's Technical Ability: Novice

Objective:
1. To explore how vibrating objects produce sound.
2. To learn about the glass armonica.
3. To use an interactive website to "play" a glass armonica.
4. To listen to a Mozart piece for glass armonica.

Materials/Equipment:
- Computer (with bookmarked sites on glass armonica, sine wave, and Ben Franklin) hooked to a TV or LCD projector.
- Glasses with water.
- Recording of a glass armonica: http://library.thinkquest.org/22254/armonica.htm.
- Ben Franklin playing the glass armonica: http://sln.fi.edu/franklin/musician/musician.html.
- Websites on the sine wave: http://www.sfu.ca/sonic-studio/handbook/Sine_Wave.html http://www.kettering.edu/~drussell/Demos.html.
- Website where you can play an interactive glass armonica: http://sln.fi.edu/franklin/musician/virtualarmonica.html.
- Website to listen to Mozart's *Adagio for Glass Harmonica*: http://www.glassarmonica.com/william/index-audio.php.

Duration: 45 minutes

Prior Knowledge and Skills: Student should know what sound is and how it is produced.

Procedure:
1. Listen to recording (on website) of a glass armonica (http://library.thinkquest.org/22254/armonica.htm).
2. Discuss: What images come to mind? Feelings? Mood?
3. Introduce glass armonica using websites on Franklin (http://sln.fi.edu/franklin/musician/musician.html).
4. Explore sound—how is it produced?

5. Use objects that create vibration/sound (*i.e.*, rubber band).
6. Using websites on the sine wave, discuss: sound waves, vibrations, etc.
   http://www.sfu.ca/sonic-studio/handbook/Sine_Wave.html
   http://www.kettering.edu/~drussell/Demos.html
7. Demonstrate/explore how glasses can produce sound:
   • Rubber mallets
   • Amount of water affecting pitch
   • Moistened fingers around rim
8. Divide class:
   • Do interactive activity "playing" the simulated glass armonica on the computers (http://sln.fi.edu/franklin/musician/virtualarmonica.html).
   • Use stem glasses to produce sound.
   • Listen to Mozart's *Adagio for Glass Harmonica* (played on stem glasses) at http://www.glassarmonica.com/william/index-audio.php.

Evaluation: Students should be able to:
1. Explain and show how sound is produced.
2. Identify the glass armonica and its origin.
3. Improvise using the interactive glass armonica and stem glasses.
4. Identify instruments played in musical listening examples.

Follow-up: You can follow up this lesson by having the students review the glass armonica and create musical pieces for the glass armonica to play for class.

Items to Be Purchased: If you have a computer or a computer lab with Internet access, then you do not need to purchase any additional items for this lesson.

Download from www.ti-me.org/TIEMC: None

MENC Standards:	6. Listening to, analyzing, and describing music.
	7. Evaluating music and musical performances.
	8. Understanding relationships between music, the other arts, and disciplines outside the arts.
	9. Understanding music in relation to history and culture.

TI:ME Technology Areas:	5. Multimedia
	6. Productivity tools/information processing/lab management
	7. Web/Internet

George Gershwin WebQuest

By Casey Hulick
Goshen Intermediate School, Goshen, New York

Grade Level:	Grade 6
Teacher's Technical Ability:	Intermediate
Objective:	Using the WebQuest Mozart quest found on the website http://www.spa3.k12.sc.us/WebQuests/mozart/travel%20log.html, the class will create a WebQuest document in Microsoft Word designed to explore the life and music of George Gershwin.
Materials/Equipment:	• Various websites.
	• Computer.
	• Projector/screen.
	• Internet access.
	• Microsoft Word (http://office.microsoft.com/en-us/default.aspx).
Duration:	120 minutes. This lesson will be a work in progress for three or four consecutive lessons.
Prior Knowledge and Skills:	This lesson is an excellent way to reinforce a unit about a specific composer.
Procedure:	1. Explore and analyze the Mozart WebQuest mentioned above. (This is to show the students an example of a good WebQuest.)
	2. Make a list of questions or tasks that we may want to answer or complete in our Gershwin quest.
	3. Search out sites focusing on the life and music of George Gershwin. Bookmark and copy the URLs that we might want to include.
	4. Gather facts and information that we might want to include along with our search for George Gershwin. Record data and links on a Microsoft Word document.
	5. Begin work on our actual Web page in Microsoft Word based on the Mozart model mentioned above—include text and appropriate Internet links where needed.

6. Copy and paste in MIDI, audio, video, or still images where appropriate.
7. Save document as an html document.
8. Preview in Web browser and review site as class. Evaluate and edit, making any desired changes, additions, deletions, or modifications as desired.
9. When complete, post on school Internet music pages website.

Evaluation: Ongoing teacher-guided group self-evaluation throughout the activity.

Follow-up: Additional WebQuest creation projects about other composers or appropriate general music topics.

Items to Be Purchased: If your school has Internet access and Microsoft Word on each computer, then you will not need to purchase any additional items for this lesson.

Download from www.ti-me.org/TIEMC: None

MENC Standards:	2. Performing on instruments, alone and with others, a varied repertoire of music.
	4. Composing and arranging music within specified guidelines.
	5. Reading and notating music.
	6. Listening to, analyzing, and describing music.
	7. Evaluating music and musical performances.
	8. Understanding relationships between music, the other arts, and disciplines outside the arts.
	9. Understanding music in relation to history and culture.
TI:ME Technology Areas:	2. Music production
	5. Multimedia

Dr. Martin Luther King, Jr.: History and Music

By Amy Vanderwall
PS 334, New York City, New York

Grade Level:	Grades 4–6
Teacher's Technical Ability:	Intermediate
Objective:	The overall goal of this activity is to have students explore a speech made by Dr. Martin Luther King, Jr., write and record musical lyrics to express their understanding of the life and work of Dr. King, and to further their understanding of this important historical figure. Students will explore their musical lyrics through the use of the SCAMPER probing questions.
Materials/Equipment:	• Chalkboard or whiteboard.
	• A copy of the "I Have a Dream" speech, delivered by Dr. Martin Luther King, Jr. on August 28, 1963, at the March on Washington for Jobs and Freedom. An electronic version can be retrieved from the Martin Luther King, Jr., Papers Project at Stanford University at: http://www.stanford.edu/group/King/publications/speechesFrame.htm. Note: this website also provides an autobiography and timeline of Dr. Martin Luther King, Jr.'s life, which is a wonderful resource.
	• Student instruments.
	• Sheet music for a song the class has already played on their instruments (see "Download from www.ti-me.org/TIEMC").
	• Paper for student journals.
	• Apple's GarageBand (http://www.apple.com/ilife/garageband/) (for Mac only, or any digital audio recording software such as Audacity (http://audacity.sourceforge.net/).
Duration:	Teachers should assess their own class needs, but projected timing is three 45-minute classes.

Prior Knowledge and Skills: This lesson should be presented to students who have a prior knowledge of the life and work of Dr. Martin Luther King, Jr. If this is not the case, this lesson should be presented in conjunction to an American history or American studies class unit on Dr. King. Furthermore, before this lesson, a music class should be dedicated to the exploration of his life allowing for student reflection and contemplation.

Procedure: **Class 1**

1. Pose the questions, "Who was Dr. Martin Luther King, Jr.?" Have students reflect on his life. Key points:
   a. Dr. Martin Luther King, Jr., is known for being one of the greatest orators of the twentieth century. He was born on January 15, 1929, and was assassinated on April 4, 1968.
   b. In the 1950s and 1960s, his words led the Civil Rights Movement and helped change society by ending racial segregation and achieving civil equality for African Americans.
   c. His ultimate goal was a large one: he hoped to achieve acceptance for all people, regardless of race or nationality, in all parts of the world.
   d. *Do not rush this discussion.* Sensitive ideas and historical realities will be discussed. If it takes the entire class, allow it.
2. Pass out the "I Have a Dream" speech to each class member. Ask for volunteers to read the speech.
3. Read the speech.
4. Ask students, "What was Dr. King saying in this speech?" Hold an in-depth discussion.
5. Ask students to take the last ten minutes of class to write in their journals about Dr. King and the "I Have a Dream" speech.

Class 2

1. Ask students to take out their journals from the last class.
2. Pass out a copy of sheet music already familiar to the students. The music does not have to have lyrics but it must possess a melody for which students could write lyrics. The music should provide for two verses of lyrics. Easy to sing and play recommendations: "When the Saints Go Marching In," "Ode to Joy," or "Twinkle, Twinkle Little Star" (see "Download from www.ti-me.org/TIEMC").
3. Ask students to write two verses of lyrics that reflect the life and work of Dr. King. Provide ten minutes for this initial exercise.
4. Write the SCAMPER approach on the board:
   > S—Substitute?
   > C—Combine?
   > A—Adapt?
   > M—Modify? Magnify?
   > P—Put in other words?
   > E—Eliminate or reduce?
   > R—Reverse? Rearrange?
5. Ask students to write SCAMPER in their journals. Ask them to revisit their lyrics, asking themselves the SCAMPER questions. In addition, they should ask themselves if the words are musical and if the words fit the rhythmic notation of the music.
6. Ask students to revise/solidify their lyrics and be sure to write out a final version in their journals. Students should then practice singing their lyrics and practice the melody on their instrument.
7. Let students know that during the next class, each student will perform their lyrics, accompanied by a group of fellow students. Journals will be collected.

Class 3

1. Provide students five minutes to get ready to perform.
2. Get ready to record their pieces:
   a. You can record them, or have them record themselves.
   b. Launch Apple's GarageBand, click on "New Music Project," title the song, click on the "+"on the bottom left corner of the screen, then finally click on "Real Instrument." This sets up the program to record live instruments.
   c. On the new track that you just created, press the red button to record their pieces. Create a new track for each piece.
   d. When they are finished, save the file.
   e. From here, you can burn the pieces to CD by clicking on "Share" and then "Send Song to iTunes." Make sure that you mute the other tracks so that you are mixing one track individually. Another option is posting them to the school's website. One way this can be done is to click on "Share" and then "Send Podcast to iWeb."
3. Put students into rotating groups of three to four. These groups will provide accompaniment for other students while they sing their lyrics. Each student will have a chance to present their lyrics and play on their instrument three to four times.
4. Have each student sing their lyrics, accompanied by other students.
5. After each student has had the chance to perform, end the session by asking, "What did you hear?" Then state that there are no right or wrong answers. Discuss the different approaches students took to representing the life and work of Dr. King.
6. Thank the group for a great experience! Collect journals.

Evaluation: This evaluation is available on the TI:ME website for print (see "Download from www.ti-me.org/TIEMC").

STUDENT
NAME:_____

Component	Possible Points	Points Given	Comments
Lyrics: Clear, reflective of the life and work of Dr. Martin Luther King, Jr.			
Journal: Reflective writing about the ideas/work of Dr. Martin Luther King, Jr.			
Journal: SCAMPER used and lyrics revised accordingly			
Music: Expression of lyrics, tone, melody			
Total			

Follow-up:

1. Have students draw/paint/sketch an image to go with their lyrics. This can be done in music class, or as a joint art class project.
2. Have students write their own "I Have a Dream" speech using similar phrasing and poetic nuances found in Dr. King's speech. This, too, can be set to music and recorded.
3. Have students compose, notate, and perform an original musical score to go with their lyrics. This, too, can be recorded.

Items to Be Purchased: This lesson requires an audio recording software. Examples of audio recording programs are the freeware Audacity (http://audacity.sourceforge.net/), for Mac or PC, or Apple's GarageBand (http://www.apple.com/ilife/garageband/), for Mac only.

Download from www.ti-me.org/TIEMC:

- "When_The_Saints_Go_Marching_In.pdf"
- "Ode_To_Joy.pdf"
- "Twinkle_Twinkle.pdf"
- "Assessment_for_Dr_King_Lesson.pdf"

MENC Standards: 6. Listening to, analyzing, and describing music.
8. Understanding relationships between music, the other arts, and disciplines outside the arts.
9. Understanding music in relation to history and culture.

TI:ME Technology Areas: 5. Multimedia
6. Productivity tools/information processing/lab management
7. Web/Internet

Creating Concert Programs

By Rosemary Nagy
JP Case Middle School, Flemington, New Jersey

Grade Level: Grade 6

Teacher's Technical Ability: Intermediate

Objective: Using Microsoft Publisher (http://office.microsoft.com/en-us/publisher/default.aspx) or a word processing program, the students will create a concert program of music featuring a baroque composer of their choice. This project will conclude the baroque component of a sixth grade general music curriculum.

Materials/Equipment:
- Overhead projector.
- Rubric to check work and compare with other student projects.
- Computer lab outfitted with Microsoft Publisher, Word (http://office.microsoft.com/en-us/default.aspx), or any word processing program.
- Internet access.
- Program cover.
- The following websites:
  http://www.baroquemusic.org/barcomp.html
  http://www.jsbach.net/bcs/
  http://www.jsbach.org/biography.html
  http://www.baroquemusic.org
  http://www.antonio-vivaldi.org
  http://www.naxos.com/composer/vivaldi.htm
  http://www.gfhandel.org/
  http://w3.rz-berlin.mpg.de/cmp/handel.html

Duration: This assignment is designed for three 80-minute block periods.

Prior Knowledge and Skills: The students should have already received information on Bach, Handel, and Vivaldi. The students will have prior experience with Publisher from their sixth grade computer class.

Procedure:

1. Ask if any students have gone to or performed in a concert. Most, if not all, will raise their hands. The teacher then asks the students to look at the program cover which will read:
   a. Name of performing group—*i.e.*, RFMS Chorale and Symphony Orchestra
   b. Works performed—*i.e.*, Ach Gott und Herr, Brandenburg Concerto No. 1, conducted by Johann Sebastian Bach
2. Ask students to consider why it would be important to have this information on a concert program. First have the students think quietly to themselves (if any students raise their hand, ask them to wait), then ask them to discuss their answers with a neighbor. After a minute or so of discussion, choose a student for an answer.
3. Pass out a project information sheet. Using Microsoft Publisher or a word processing program, students then create a concert program with the following information on it:
   a. Cover page (page 1): Picture of baroque composer of their choice. Must have composer's name and dates as well as the date of the actual concert, name of performing group(s), and place the concert is held.
   b. Page 2: Brief biography of the composer including where he was born and died.
   c. Page 3: Program of six songs. The students may include an intermission.
   d. Page 4: The students will use this page to cite all works on their programs.
4. They may also use any extra clip art or pictures relevant to their composers.
5. Briefly review Publisher and answers any student questions.
6. The students then choose their composers and begin working on the project.

Evaluation:

1. Check for student understanding:
   a. You will know if students are struggling by observing their progress on the computer.
   b. The students should have accurate information on composers, etc.
2. Closure:
   a. The students will be placed into groups of four to present and compare projects.
   b. They will use a rubric to critique each other as well as evaluate their own projects.
   c. For great rubric ideas and designs go to: http://rubistar.4teachers.org/index.php.

Follow-up: The students can complete this unit with a student talk show. Students will choose who will play the composer and who will be the talk show host. They write a script containing basic information on their composers and perform in class for each other.

Students could also create a short Microsoft PowerPoint (http://office.microsoft.com/en-us/powerpoint/default.aspx) presentation, possibly with an audio clip of their composer's music.

Items to Be Purchased: Most schools' computers are equipped with a word processing program. Therefore, no items need to be purchased.

Download from www.ti-me.org/TIEMC: None

MENC Standards:	6. Listening to, analyzing, and describing music.
	8. Understanding relationships between music, the other arts, and disciplines outside the arts.
TI:ME Technology Areas:	5. Multimedia

Physics of Sound: Timbre

By Thomas Berdos
Pingry School, Lower School, Short Hills, New Jersey

Grade Level:	Grades 5–6
Teacher's Technical Ability:	Novice
Objective:	Students will explore the concept of timbre by verbal, aural, and visual means, comparing the timbre of various musical instruments and different human voices.
Materials/Equipment:	• Acoustic instruments such as oboe, trumpet, recorder, clarinet, flute, and so forth. You need only to play the tuning pitch on these instruments. Since this lesson is for grades 5 and 6, you can also have the students play various pitches on their own instruments.
	• Oscilloscope—a device that uses a cathode ray tube to produce a visualization of an electrical current on a screen. For this lesson, the oscilloscope is software that is loaded onto a computer. The one used in this lesson can be found here: http://www.electronics-lab.com/downloads/pc/001/ (for PC only). Another example of an oscilloscope can be found here: http://www.picotech.com/demo.html (for PC only). There is an oscilloscope software free from Mac called "Mac the Scope": http://www.channld.com/dwnldpg.html.
	• Computer hooked to a TV or LCD projector and projected onto a screen.
Duration:	30–40 minutes
Prior Knowledge and Skills:	The students have prior knowledge of the concept of timbre (the quality of tone).
Procedure:	1. Review concept of timbre.
	2. Play an A (440 Hz) on the oboe, then the same pitch (B) on a B♭ cornet.
	3. Have students list adjectives to describe the sound of each (but *not* comparisons... their adjectives should be more abstract than "cat-like," etc.).
	4. Play sample notes several more times while students read lists of words.
	5. Play each sound into the oscilloscope (see Fig. 3.5).

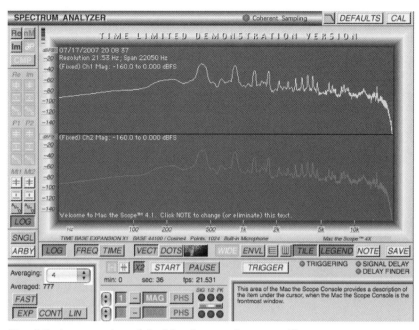

Fig. 3.5: A screen shot of the Mac Scope software oscilloscope.

6. Trace the sound wave onto the blackboard.
7. Discuss the shape of the sound, and compare it to the adjectives.
8. Have students sing the same pitch into the oscilloscope.
9. Trace their sound waves onto the blackboard.
10. Compare student voices to each other and to the instruments.
11. Which instrument is more voice-like, and why?

Evaluation: Students will be able to distinguish between different timbres. They will make associations between the audible timbre and the visual shape of the sound wave. They will draw comparisons concerning timbre between instruments and voices.

Follow-up: Follow-up activities could include:
1. Students and teacher agree on a list of adjectives for a desired timbre at A (440 Hz). Students design the sound wave for that timbre based this lesson.
2. Band students explore timbre by playing each other's parts (for example, the clarinet plays the trumpet part, and vice versa), and discussing instrumentation.
3. Chorus students consider the timbre of voices in the chorus, enabling them to understand the concept of choral blend.

Items to Be Purchased: An oscilloscope is required for this lesson. This can be purchased or downloaded for free as software from the websites listed under the "Materials/Equipment" section.

Download from www.ti-me.org/TIEMC: None

MENC Standards:	2. Performing on instruments, alone and with others, a varied repertoire of music.
	6. Listening to, analyzing, and describing music.
	8. Understanding relationships between music, the other arts, and disciplines outside the arts.
TI:ME Technology Areas:	2. Music production
	4. Instructional music software

Understanding Waveforms by Generating Sustained Tones
By Jon Boyle
Rose Tree Media School District, Media, Pennsylvania

Grade Level:	Grades 3–6
Teacher's Technical Ability:	Intermediate
Objective:	1. Students will correlate visual information in a digital audio recorder to sound information.
	2. Students will manipulate their sound and visual data in the digital audio recording software to look and sound a specific way.
	3. Students will learn this manipulation relates directly to dynamic information found in music.
Materials/Equipment:	• Computer with digital audio recording software that allows users to view waveform data of their recordings graphically. If your computer does not have a digital audio software, Audacity (http://audacity.sourceforge.net/), a freeware digital audio program, can be used on either PC or Mac.
	• Instruments that can generate a long sound:
	Recorders
	Voice
	Woodwinds
	Strings
	Brass instruments
Duration:	20 minutes
Prior Knowledge and Skills:	The students must be able to generate a long, steady tone on their instrument.
Procedure:	1. Play a long, sustained tone and record it in a digital audio recording application such as Audacity.
	2. Show the graphic representation or waveform of this sound byte.
	3. Play the sustained tone again, this time with a *crescendo*.

4. You and the students observe and discuss the difference visual and audio aspects of the two sound bytes.

5. The students record their own sustained tones both with and without *crescendos*. Analyze and discuss the waveforms of these sound bytes.

6. The students have multiple attempts to change their waveform and sound to represent a true *crescendo*.

Evaluation:

1. The teacher can have the visual and audio data of each student's sound files.

2. Students are given instant feedback from the visual and audio data in the program.

Follow-up:

Record live performances and analyze the dynamics visually and audibly.

Students can record melodies with dynamic changes and analyze their own performance.

The lesson can be expanded to include accents, *staccato/legato*, timbre, tone.

Items to Be Purchased:

Computer with digital audio recording capabilities, such as an audio interface or a built-in internal microphone.

If you already have a computer in your classroom, and you download the freeware digital audio program Audacity (http://audacity.sourceforge.net/), then you will not need to purchase any items. More powerful digital audio programs can be purchased.

Download from www.ti-me.org/TIEMC:

None

Glossary

12-bar blues progression: A chord progression of I–I–I–I–IV–IV–I–I–V–IV–I–I

Adobe Flash: A software program used to design and author interactive websites or subject matter that includes video, graphics, and animation. For Mac and PC. http://www.adobe.com/products/flashplayer/

Apple GarageBand: GarageBand includes professionally prerecorded rhythm sections, solos, loops, and instrumental performances that act like "virtual musicians," which you conduct to create custom songs. GarageBand is a part of Apple's iLife software. For Mac only. http://www.apple.com/ilife/garageband/

Apple iPod: A portable media player manufactured by Apple. For Mac and PC. http://www.apple.com/itunes/

Apple iTunes: A free, digital media application that is offered by Apple. For Mac or PC. http://www.apple.com/itunes/

Apple Keynote: A presentation program a part of Apple's iWorks. For Mac only. http://www.apple.com/iwork/keynote/

Audacity: A free, cross-platform (Mac or PC), easy-to-use audio editor and recorder that can be used to record live audio, convert tapes and records into digital recordings or CDs, edit MP3 or WAV files, edit sound files, and change pitch and speed of a recording. http://audacity.sourceforge.net/

augmentation: Extending or lengthening the rhythm of a melody.

bordun: A term usually found in the Orff-Schulwerk methodology, when one plays the first and fifth tones of the scale together on an Orff instrument.

Cakewalk Sonar Home Studio: Software that records numerous tracks of audio and MIDI. For PC only. http://www.cakewalk.com/Products/HomeStudio/default.asp

call and response: When one group sings a melody first (call) and another group sings a melody second (response).

CD: Compact disc.

CD burning: A compact disc drive that is able to produce a disc that can be read by other audio players.

CD or DVD drive: A drive for using CD-ROM software or for playing audio compact disks. DVD-ROM drives can read information from a DVD and will also play all CD-ROM software and audio CDs.

computer-assisted instruction (CAI): Instructional software that incorporates technology to serve as a tutor, tool, or tutee. There is no universal term for this. CAI serves as an umbrella for several interchangeable terms including computer-assisted instruction in music and computer-based music instruction (Rudolph, 2004, pp. 115–116).

creative, practice, and performance software: Auto-accompaniment software that is capable of recording one track of MIDI and one track of audio.

Digidesign Pro Tools: A digital audio workstation for music production and digital audio editing. http://www.digidesign.com

digital audio: Sound recording storing, and editing with discrete values (a string of amplitude samples) as opposed to analog, or continuous values. Common digital audio formats include AIFF, WAV, and MP3.

diminution: Compressing the rhythm of a melody.

DVD: Digital video disc.

Elmo: A digital visual presenter that allows you to present images of virtually anything to anyone at any time, with the assistance of a projector.

Finale, Finale Allegro, Finale PrintMusic, Finale Songwriter, and Finale NotePad: A variety of notation programs for composing, arranging, teaching, and publishing music, put out by MakeMusic. For Mac or PC. http://www.finalemusic.com/finale/

freeware: A copyrighted computer software that is free for use.

graphic editor in a sequencing program: A sequencing program will often give you the option to view the notes in the graphic editor as opposed to standard notation. It looks like a "piano roll"—a roll of paper with perforations punched in it. The position and length of the graphic line determines the note played on the piano.

Group Education Controller: The Korg Group Education Controller (GEC3—the 3 denotes that this is the third edition) networks the room to produce a controlled group atmosphere for keyboard instruction. http://www.korg.com/gear/info.asp?A_PROD_NO=GEC3

haiku: A 17-syllable verse form consisting of three metrical units of five, seven, and five syllables.

Harmonic Vision's Music Ace Maestro: Forty-eight engaging, self-paced lessons that accelerate development and reinforce fundamental music skills and an understanding of music theory. For Mac or PC. http://www.harmonicvision.com/

International Society for Technology in Education (ISTE): Organization that provides leadership and service to improve teaching, learning, and school leadership by advancing the effective use of technology in pre-K–12 and teacher education. http://www.iste.org/

Internet: A worldwide system of interconnected computer networks.

Intuem: A MIDI, audio, and ReWire music authoring environment. For Mac only.

keyboard lab resources:
- *Finding Funds for Music Technology* by Tom Rudolph, SoundTree, 1999.
- SoundTree, music technology services for education: http://www.soundtree.com/welcome.asp
- Yamaha Music in Education, a technology-based music program: http://www.mus-central.com/MIE.htm

looping: The process of playing back data repeatedly.

M-Audio MicroTrack: A two-channel WAV and MP3 recording and playback device for pro recording, meetings, training, education, and worship. http://www.m-audio.com

microphone: Some computers have internal, built-in microphones while others need to have an external microphone connected to the sound-in jack of the computer.

Microsoft PowerPoint: A presentation program that is part of the Microsoft Office suite. For PC or Mac. http://office.microsoft.com

MIDI: An acronym for the Musical Instrument Digital Interface, a software and hardware protocol that allows electronic musical instruments and computers to communicate with each other.

MOTU (Mark of the Unicorn) Digital Performer: Sequencing and audio software program. http://www.motu.com

MP3: An acronym for MPEG-1 (Moving Pictures Experts Group) Layer 3, a digitally encoded, compressed audio format.

.mus file: The extension of a Finale file.

Music Education Technology **magazine:** *MET Magazine*, a property of Penton Media, is a quarterly publication (September, December, March, and June). The emphasis is on providing clear and straight-forward technical solutions for music teachers. http://metmagazine.com/

music notation software: Software used to create, compose, and print sheet music (Finale and Sibelius are examples).

music production software: Software that records multiple tracks of audio and MIDI (MOTU's Digital Performer and Apple's GarageBand are examples).

National Association for Music Education (MENC) national standards:
(http://www.menc.org/publication/books/standards.htm):
1. Singing, alone and with others, a varied repertoire of music.
2. Performing on instruments, alone and with others, a varied repertoire of music.
3. Improvising melodies, variations, and accompaniments.
4. Composing and arranging music within specified guidelines.
5. Reading and notating music.
6. Listening to, analyzing, and describing music.
7. Evaluating music and music performances.
8. Understanding relationships between music, the other arts, and disciplines outside the arts.
9. Understanding music in relation to history and culture.

oscilloscope: A device that uses a cathode ray tube to produce a visualization of an electrical current on a screen.

parallel period: A period in which the second phrase is a repetition, modified repetition, or a variant of the first phrase.

PDF (Portable Document Format) file: A universal file format that preserves the fonts, images, graphics, and layout of any document regardless of computer and platform types; requires Adobe's Acrobat Reader to be viewed.

PG Music's Band-in-a-Box: Auto-accompaniment software for Mac or PC. http://www.pgmusic.com/

podcast: A media file circulated by subscription.

podcasting: A portmanteau of Apple's "iPod" and "broadcasting," podcasting is a method of publishing files to the Internet, and allowing users to subscribe to a feed for receiving new files automatically by subscription, usually at no cost. First reaching popularity in late 2004, it is used largely for audio files.

project-based learning: The process of actively engaging students in an authentic experience that will have benefits and consequences.

question-and-answer phrasing: A two-phrase melody that includes the first phrase ending on any pitch that is not tonic, and the second phrase ending on the tonic pitch.

retrograde: In reverse order; could apply to performance or composition of a melody.

round: A song in which voices follow each other; one voice starts and others join in one after another until all are singing different parts of the song at the same time.

scanner: A device that converts visual information into digital data.

sequencer: A software or hardware device made for recording, playing, and editing digital music data.

sequencing software: Software that plays or records music with a sequencer.

.sib file: The extension of a Sibelius file.

Sibelius: A software program for writing, playing, printing, and publishing music notation.

Sibelius's Groovy Music series: A series of three exciting, computer-assisted instructional software programs for elementary school students ranging in ages from five to eleven. It aids in teaching the basics of sound, rhythm, pitch, and composition by using pictures and animation. Groovy Shapes is for ages 5–7, Groovy Jungle is for ages 7–9, and Groovy City is for ages 9–11. For Mac or PC. http://www.sibelius.com/products/groovy/index.html

Smart Board: An interactive white board system. http://www2.smarttech.com/st/en-US/Products/SMART+Boards/default.htm

Sony Acid Music Studio or Acid Pro: A loop-based, audio-editing software program. For PC only. http://www.sonymediasoftware.com

Steinberg Cubase: A digital audio workstation for MIDI, music sequencing, and digital audio editing. For Mac and PC. http://www.steinberg.net/

teaching music "on a cart": When a music teacher teaches music in the student's classroom, or other classrooms, as opposed to teaching music in a music classroom.

WebQuest: A project that utilizes websites to help students develop analytical and decision-making skills.

XtremeMac MicroMemo: Device for turning the video iPod and iPod Nano into a portable, pocket-sized recording studio. http://www.xtrememac.com

References

Burns, A. *Music Technology Will Enhance Composition Skills in Grade Two.* Unpublished manuscript, August 2006.

Hickey, M. Efficiency and transformation: "The Impact of Technology on Music Education." A response to Carlesta Spearman's article "How Will Societal and Technological Changes Affect the Teaching of Music?" Vision 2020: The Housewright Symposium on the future of music education. In E. Pontiff & A. Keating (Eds.), *Spotlight on Technology in the Music Classroom*, 106–110. Reston, VA: The National Association for Music Education, 2002.

Reese, S., K. McCord, & K. Walls (eds.). *Strategies for Teaching Technology.* Reston, VA: The National Association for Music Education, 2001.

Rudolph, T. *Teaching Music with Technology* (2nd ed.). Chicago: GIA Publications, Inc., 2004.

Rudolph, T. J., F. Richmond, D. Mash, & D. Williams. *Technology Strategies for Music Education.* Wyncote, PA: The Technology Institute for Music Educators, 1997.

Stauffer, S. L., & J. Davidson (eds.). *Strategies for Teaching K–4 General Music.* Reston, VA: The National Association for Music Education, 1996.

Swearingen, K. D. "A Philosophy and Strategies for Technology in Music Education." In E. Pontiff & A. Keating (eds.), *Spotlight on Technology in the Music Classroom*, 114–116. Reston, VA: The National Association for Music Education, 2003.

Webster, P. R. "Computer-Based Technology and Music Teaching and Learning." In R. Cowell & C. Richardson (eds.), *The New Handbook of Research on Music Teaching and Learning*, 416–439. New York: Oxford University Press, 2002.

About TI:ME

The Technology Institute for Music Educators (TI:ME) is a nonprofit corporation registered in the state of Pennsylvania whose mission is to assist music educators in applying technology to improve teaching and learning in music. From the TI:ME website:

> TI:ME has published the book titled *Technology Strategies for Music Education* (second edition), written by Thomas E. Rudolph, Floyd Richmond, David Mash, Peter Webster, William I. Bauer, and Kim Walls, edited by Floyd Richmond, and published by Hal Leonard Corporation (2002). This publication is meant to be an overview. It is not a course of study, it is not meant to be a textbook, and it does not represent a full description of the curriculum or courses endorsed by TI:ME. This updated edition contains hundreds of ideas to assist teachers in integrating technology into the music curriculum, the areas of competency leading to TI:ME certification, and a description of the Technology Institute for Music Educators. These "strategies" are organized around seven essential areas of competency in music technology as they apply to the National Standards for Arts of Education. http://www.ti-me.org

TI:ME Technological Areas:
1. Electronic instruments
   - Keyboards
   - Controllers (other)
   - Synthesizers and samplers
   - Ensemble performance
2. Music production
   - Data types:
     MIDI
     Digital audio
   - Processes:
     Looping
     Sequencing
     Signal processing
     Sound design
3. Notation software
4. Instructional music software
   - Instructional software
   - Accompaniment/practice tools
   - Internet-based learning
5. Multimedia
   - Multimedia authoring:
     Web pages
     Presentations (PowerPoint, Keynote)
     Movie/DVD
   - Digital image capturing (scanning, still/video camera)
   - Internet
   - Electronic portfolios (*e.g.*, Note Taker)
6. Productivity tools/information processing/lab management
   - Productivity tools (text editor, spreadsheet, database, etc.)
   - Computer systems (CPU, I/O devices, storage devices/media, etc.)
   - Lab management systems (Korg, Roland, Lentines, etc.)
   - Networks (network manager software, server, etc.)
7. Web/Internet (outdated tech area from *Strategies* text 1st edition)

Index

National Standards for Music Education
Lessons listed by page number:

TI:ME Technology Areas
Lessons listed by page number:

Grade Level
Lessons listed by page number:

Pre-K/Kindergarten	2, 4, 7, 9, 21, 32, 34, 37, 41, 89, 92, 95, 97, 99, 103, 107, 112, 115, 120
Grade 1	4, 7, 9, 19, 21, 32, 34, 37, 41, 49, 62, 89, 92, 95, 97, 99, 103, 107, 109, 113, 115, 120
Grade 2	4, 7, 19, 21, 23, 32, 34, 37, 41, 43, 45, 47, 49, 60, 62, 65, 68, 89, 92, 95, 97, 99, 103, 107, 115, 120
Grade 3	11, 19, 21, 23, 25, 28, 34, 37, 43, 45, 47, 49, 52, 54, 56, 60, 62, 65, 68, 89, 92, 95, 97, 99, 103, 107, 120, 134
Grade 4	11, 13, 19, 21, 23, 25, 28, 34, 37, 43, 45, 47, 52, 54, 56, 58, 60, 65, 68, 71, 73, 75, 89, 92, 95, 97, 99, 103, 107, 118, 120, 126, 134
Grade 5	11, 13, 16, 19, 21, 28, 30, 34, 37, 43, 45, 47, 52, 54, 56, 58, 65, 68, 71, 73, 75, 78, 81, 86, 89, 92, 95, 97, 99, 103, 107, 122, 126, 132, 134
Grade 6	11, 13, 16, 19, 28, 30, 34, 37, 43, 45, 52, 54, 58, 71, 73, 75, 78, 81, 86, 89, 92, 95, 97, 99, 103, 107, 124, 126, 130, 132, 134

Teacher's Technical Ability
Lessons listed by page number:

Novice	2, 9, 11, 13, 19, 21, 23, 25, 41, 43, 45, 47, 49, 56, 60, 71, 75, 109, 112, 113, 115, 120, 122, 132
Intermediate	4, 7, 13, 16, 28, 30, 32, 34, 37, 52, 54, 56, 58, 62, 65, 71, 73, 81, 107, 124, 126, 130, 134
Advanced	7, 68, 78, 86, 89, 92, 95, 97, 99, 103, 118

Lessons with Files on the TI:ME Website
Lessons listed by page number:

2, 4, 11, 16, 19, 23, 25, 30, 34, 45, 47, 52, 56, 58, 60, 62, 65, 68, 71, 73, 78, 81, 89, 99, 107, 109, 115, 118, 126

About the Contributors

Amy M. Burns holds a bachelor of music in both education and performance from Ithaca College and a master of science in music education from Central Connecticut State University, with her capstone research project focusing on composition with music technology at the second grade level. She also holds TI:ME levels 1 and 2 certification as well as Orff level 1 certification and Kodály level 1 certification. For the past eleven years, Ms. Burns has taught general music to grades pre-Kindergarten through three, directed the instrumental band, the flute and clarinet ensembles, the elementary choruses, and coordinated the after-school conservatory for Far Hills Country Day School, in Far Hills, New Jersey. She has presented workshops on integrating music technology into the elementary music classroom for district and state conferences in New Jersey, Florida, Massachusetts, Pennsylvania, Connecticut, New York, and Texas. Ms. Burns has also presented sessions at the 2004 and 2006 national conferences for Technology Institute for Music Educators (TI:ME); the 2006 National Association for Music Education (MENC) national conference in Salt Lake City, Utah; and the 2007 MENC eastern divisional conference in Hartford, Connecticut. She has contributed lesson plans to SoundTree's Educator Corner and has written articles for the TI:ME website, the TI:ME newsletter, SoundTree Resource News, MENC *General Music Today*, NJMEA *Tempo*, and *Music Education Technology* (MET) magazine. In 2005, Ms. Burns was awarded the first-ever TI:ME Teacher of the Year Award in recognition of her outstanding achievements in integrating music technology into the elementary classroom.

Anna Anderson started her music studies just before turning five. Soon after, her parents brought her to a piano teacher for private lessons. At the age of 6, she began to play the violin and piano, and was accepted to a special music school for gifted children in Kiev, Ukraine. She immigrated to the United States and completed high school in Brooklyn, New York, where she studied violin, as well as other music subjects with Nannette Levi Harry at the Mannes College of Music prep division. Ms. Anderson received her BA and MA in music education with a concentration in violin from Boston University in 2001 and 2003, respectively. She is now teaching general music, chorus, and strings in the public schools of Massachusetts, as well as private lessons.

Tom Berdos teaches general music, chorus, and instrumental music to students in grades 4–6, as well as faculty music ensembles, at the Pingry School in Short Hills, New Jersey. He also serves as Director of Music Ministries at First Presbyterian Church, Mendham, New Jersey. Tom earned the bachelor of music degree in music education and the master of music degree in piano performance from the University of Lowell. In addition to his teaching at Pingry, Tom has taught piano, music history, and other music courses at a number of colleges, and has performed as a pianist in the U.S. and abroad. Tom has also served as guest conductor at the Ocean Grove Choir Festival in Ocean Grove, New Jersey, on several occasions.

Jon Boyle, a TI:ME member, resides in Havertown, Pennsylvania, with his wife, Michele. He is the elementary band director at Indian Lane Elementary and Rose Tree Elementary in the Rose Tree Media school district. He received his master's in music technology from Indiana University-Perdue University Indianapolis (IUPUI), and a bachelor's in music from Temple University.

Carol Childers earned a bachelor of music education degree from Youngstown State University and a master of library science degree from Kent State University. She taught band for one year in the Youngstown (Ohio) Diocese. She taught elementary music in the Youngstown city schools for 20 years. She is currently the school librarian and media specialist at Hayes Middle School in Youngstown, Ohio. Carol also has taught private bassoon lessons for over 15 years. In addition, she has played with the following musical groups: Youngstown Symphony Orchestra, Warren Chamber Orchestra, Greenville Symphony, Ashtabula Symphony, W.D. Packard Concert Band, Edelweiss Woodwind Quartet, The 5 Winds Woodwind Quintet, and her church's praise band. She has conducted the vocal ensemble for her church's passion play the past three years.

Kelly Conlon grew up in North Smithfield, Rhode Island. She has played flute and piccolo in a number of collegiate and professional venues throughout the New England area. She earned a bachelor of science degree in music education from Rhode Island College in 2002. Currently, she teaches elementary music in Smithfield, Rhode Island, where she directs a band, chorus, and recorder program. In her spare time Kelly teaches private instrument and dance instruction.

Christine Dunleavy teaches general music at Winslow Township Upper Elementary School #5 in Camden County, New Jersey, where she also directs the third grade and fourth/fifth grade choruses. In addition to teaching, she is the piano accompanist for the district elementary orchestra. She has served as a teaching mentor and is presently a representative on the district's instructional council. A graduate of the University of Maryland at College Park, she received her master's degree in music (voice) from Temple University, and is a frequent soprano soloist with several Delaware Valley professional groups: most recently Voces Novae et Antiquae (VNA), the West Jersey Chamber Society, and the Bach Festival of Philadelphia. Ms. Dunleavy has also appeared as soloist with Pennsylvania Pro Musica, the Germantown Oratorio Choir, First Presbyterian Church of Moorestown, Laurel Oratorio Society, Opera Society of New Jersey, Choristers of Upper Dublin, and the Shakespeare Festival Musicale. An accomplished singer of contemporary music, Ms. Dunleavy premiered the winning selection at the Long Island Composers Alliance Concert and was guest soloist at the Concert of New Music by Temple Composers.

Matthew Etherington has lived and worked in the United States since moving from England in 2002. He holds a bachelor's degree with honors in jazz studies from the University of Leeds, a master's degree in composition for film and television, and a post-graduate certificate in education from the University of Bristol. Matthew held the post of lower school director of music for three years at Milton Academy in Milton, Massachusetts, and is currently the performing arts department head at Camelot Academy in Durham, North Carolina. Over the past ten years, Matthew has performed on piano, keyboards, saxophone, and percussion in Europe, South Africa, and the United States. In 2004, he co-directed a school performance at an award ceremony for Archbishop Desmond Tutu and Danny Glover. His school experience includes choral direction, musical theater, jazz groups, and music technology programs. In 2005, Matthew achieved level 3 Orff certification from the University of Memphis where he studied under Prof. Jos Wuytack. Matthew has contributed educational materials to the British Educational Communications and Technology Agency (BECTA) and to the TI:ME (Technology Institute for Music Educators) database. He is a current member of TI:ME and the creator of the music education resource Music4Education.com.

Steven Estrella earned a Ph.D. in music education from Temple University, a master of arts degree in music composition from Claremont graduate school, and a bachelor of arts in music and psychology from Eckerd College. For ten years, Dr. Estrella served as assistant professor of music education and director of computer/media services for Temple University's Boyer College of Music. He is an active member of the National Advisory Board for the Technology Institute for Music Educators (TI:ME) and has served as vice-president of TI:ME. He owns Shearspire, Inc., and StevenEstrella.com, which provide Web and media development services to clients in education and business. He has completed large interactive media projects for clients such as the Berklee College of Music, the International Music Products Association, the International Association of Electronic Keyboard Manufacturers, Addison-Wesley Publishing, McGraw-Hill Higher Education, and MacMillan. Dr. Estrella is the author of three textbooks: *The Web Wizard's Guide to Javascript, The Web Wizard's Guide to Dynamic HTML,* and *Study Outline and Workbook in the Fundamentals of Music.* His current professional passion involves creating highly interactive media to teach practical skills and concepts in music and other disciplines.

Karen L. Garrett, the 2006 TI:ME Teacher of the Year, teaches elementary music technology and band at Central Park Elementary School in Birmingham, Alabama. She has been teaching in the Birmingham city school system since 1992. She has presented sessions at the national TI:ME conference and the Alabama Music Educators Association, as well as sessions to music teachers in the Birmingham area. Her music technology website is www.musictechteacher.com, which features many quizzes, worksheets, lessons, and student work, along with information about using technology to teach music. Ms. Garrett may be contacted at kgarrett@musictechteacher.com.

Robin Hansen has taught music at all levels in the school district of Chatham, New Jersey, for the past 23 years. She is currently in the Lafayette School where her fourth and fifth grade choruses each contain 220 members. A 16-station music technology lab was installed in 2003, and Mrs. Hansen has used this tool with her fourth and fifth grade general music classes to enhance the curriculum. Students have used several music programs with the iMacs and Korg X5Ds, including Harmonic Vision's Music Ace, PG Music's Band-in-a-Box, and Apple's GarageBand.

Casey Hulick received a B.A. degree in music education from Trenton State College in New Jersey in 1976 and an M.A. in music from Western State College in Gunnison, Colorado in 1979. He has 28 years' experience in music education. Currently, Mr. Hulick teaches vocal and general music at Goshen Intermediate School (GIS) in Goshen, New York. Mr. Hulick is a member of TI:ME and is level 2 certified. Mr. Hulick created a special music website for the GIS music program, which also features a "kid friendly" music activities page with many fine music links, and an even more extensive links page designed for anybody. His website is located at http://goshenschoolsny.org/Schools/GIS/Websites/SpecialAreas/CHulick/index.htm.

Madean Kramer teaches general music to grades 4–7 at Far Hills Country Day School, in Far Hills, New Jersey. In addition, she teaches eighth grade music electives and directs the Falconnaires, a grades 6–8 vocal ensemble. A graduate of Pennsylvania State University, Maedean has taught vocal music at Simsbury High School and Westminster School in Simsbury, Connecticut, and the Purnell School in Pottersville, New Jersey. She also performs regularly with the Triad Vocal Ensemble. Currently, Ms. Kramer is a member of NJMEA and MENC. In addition, she has presented music technology workshops for the New Jersey Association for Independent Schools (NJAIS).

Stefani Langol is a music educator, clinician, author, and consultant. She is currently assistant professor of music education at Berklee College of Music and serves as the technology coordinator for the department. In addition, Stefani is a member of the Technology Institute for Music Educators (TI:ME) National Advisory Board, and served as editor-in-chief of the TI:ME's newsletter from 1997 to 2004.

Don Muro (www.donmuro.com) began experimenting with tape recorders as a child and has maintained an intense interest and enthusiasm for electronic music composition, performance, recording, and teaching. His compositions have embraced several musical styles including sacred, classical, rock, and fusion. He has been the recipient of several ASCAP composition awards, and his music has been performed in settings ranging from London's St. Paul's Cathedral to Disneyland. His educational music is widely used throughout the United States, as well as in Europe and in Japan. His demonstration compositions for the legendary Korg M1 helped to make it the world's best-selling music workstation.

Don has been an active advocate for music technology. In addition to producing two videos, he has written four books for the Music Expressions Music Technology/MIDI Keyboard Curriculum (Alfred). He is a contributing author of the *Technology Guide for Music Educators* (Thompson). He has also written more than eighty articles about music and technology for publications such as *International Musician, The Instrumentalist, Keyboard, Music Educators Journal, Music Education Technology*, and *The American Organist*. He served as a contributor to the New York State Education Department and as a member of the National Association for the Music Education (MENC) Technology Task Force which produced the *Opportunity-to-Learn Standards for Music Technology*. He was the first chairman of electronic music for both International Association for Jazz Educators (IAJE) and New York State School Music Association (NYSSMA), as well as one of the founding members of TI:ME. Don is currently the music director for the Electronic Arts Foundation, a columnist for *Music Education Technology*, and a member for both the TI:ME board of directors and the NYSSMA technology committee.

Rosemary Nagy is one of the vocal music teachers at the J. P. Case Middle School in Flemington, New Jersey. During her tenure at Flemington, she was nominated as the 2002 Teacher of the Year and received the New Jersey Governor's Teacher Recognition Award. Rose is also a Fulbright Alumnus, teaching in Sherborne, England, during the spring of 2004. Her choirs have received numerous first-place, superior, and best-overall ensemble awards and she has been a guest conductor for the Central Jersey Music Educators Region II Honors Chorus. Rose received her bachelor of music degree from Westminster Choir College and has a master of arts degree from Teachers College, Columbia University, where she was inducted into Kappa Delta Pi, the education honors society.

Susan Jannery Nichols is a graduate of the University of New Hampshire in music education. She has taken additional classes in music technology, differentiated instruction, curriculum design, information systems, and various business courses. Susan began her teaching career in Exeter, New Hampshire. She then spent many years as a programmer/analyst for Connecticut manufacturing firms until resuming her teaching career in Bedford and now Amherst, New Hampshire, at the Amherst Middle School. There she teaches band, chorus, and general music classes. She relies on the use of technology for accompanying choruses in rehearsal, creating MP3 files for the school website in order for her band and chorus students to practice at home, and for the generation of written instructional materials for her students as well as for performance assessment. She is the proud mother of three great teenagers, and has been married to her husband, Brad, for 22 years.

Thomas Rudolph (www.tomrudolph.com), Ed. D., is the director of music for Haverford School District, in Havertown, Pennsylvania, and an adjunct assistant professor at the University of the Arts. He teaches technology courses at Berklee College of Music, Central Connecticut State University, and Villanova University. Tom is the president of TI:ME, the Technology Institute for Music Educators. His books include, *Sibelius: A Comprehensive Guide, Finale: An Easy Guide to Music Notation, Recording in the Digital World,* and *Teaching Music with Technology.* His articles have appeared in the *Music Educators Journal, The Instrumentalist, Jazz Educator Journal, DownBeat* magazine, and *Music Education Technology* magazine.

Maureen Spranza has been teaching music for ten years in the San Lorenzo Unified School District. She is currently teaching grades 1–5 band, choir, and strings at Hillside Elementary in San Leandro. She has over 19 years of teaching experience in music, including working at numerous schools in the San Lorenzo Unified School District. Maureen earned her MFA at Mills College in electronic music and recording media with an emphasis in composition. She has a bachelor's degree in music in jazz composition from Berklee College of Music in Boston. Her teaching credential is from Chapman University in Concord, and she is currently working on her comprehensive examinations for her Ph.D. in education from http://www.capella.edu with a specialization in designing online instruction. Ms. Spranza especially enjoys using project-based learning in her curriculum design. Following a mainly constructivist philosophy, she uses a learner-centered environment when possible and a pragmatic rationale. She loves to incorporate technology into the curriculum and feels lucky to work in a district that is a Microsoft Center of Excellence. She has presented educational workshops and has published articles for teachers. She has been listed in *Who's Who in America, Who's Who Among American Women, Who's Who of American Education,* and the *International Who's Who Among Professional Educators.*

Amy Vanderwall is an upper-elementary and middle school music teacher in Manhattan, and is currently in the doctoral program in music education at Teacher's College, Columbia University. In 2005, Ms. Vanderwall's school received a VH1 Save the Music grant for an electronic keyboard lab, and other grant and parent funding provided for a teacher laptop, LCD projector, MIDI cords, and other music technology tools. Since this time, Ms. Vanderwall has hosted and led numerous keyboard and music technology training sessions in conjunction with VH1 Save the Music, SoundTree, Teachers College, Columbia University, and New York City public schools with the hopes of expanding the integration of music technology into urban music classrooms. Ms. Vanderwall teaches a diverse population of learners, including students in a citywide gifted program, and has only limited music time with each student (approximately 50 minutes per week per student). Music technology has enabled Ms. Vanderwall to maximize music class time by supporting enhanced classroom management and high-impact lessons, while enabling her to more easily differentiate the curriculum to meet individual student needs and musical talents. Most importantly, music technology has elevated and energized student, administration, and parent excitement for music education in her school!

Eileen Wolpert received her bachelor's degree from Chestnut Hill College. She is currently the fine arts coordinator for Ancillae Assumpta Academy in Wyncote, Pennsylvania. In addition, she is a cellist for the string quartet Classic Strings.